Expeditions in Your Classroom
English Language Arts
for Common Core State Standards, Grades 6–8

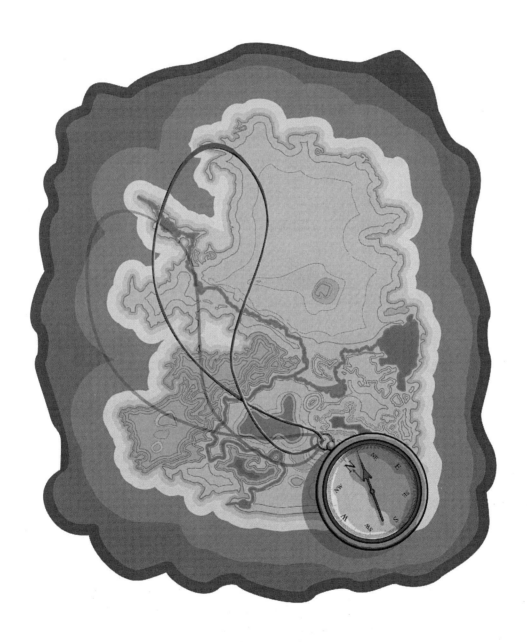

Henrietta List

1   2   3   4   5   6   7   8   9   10
ISBN 978-0-8251-6891-8
Copyright © 2009, 2012
J. Weston Walch, Publisher
40 Walch Drive • Portland, ME 04103
www.walch.com
Printed in the United States of America

Contents

Introduction

Students learn effectively when they have an opportunity to apply their knowledge to real-life problems. This book contains ten expeditions that engage students in real learning. Each project links students to a bigger issue in their community. They illustrate to students how their education has relevance in their lives today and in the future. Each expedition strives to give students new skills that can help them both inside and outside the English language arts classroom. Many projects reach out to other content areas within a student's grade level, allowing students to exchange knowledge between English language arts, social studies, and art.

Expeditions in Your Classroom: English Language Arts for Common Core State Standards, Grades 6–8 is designed for middle-school students. It provides activities and materials that scaffold student tasks; sets clear criteria for final products; and offers assessment tools and a detailed outline of project steps so that teachers can focus energy on instruction rather than on project management. Each expedition addresses national standards and provides accessible routes to understanding for a broad audience of students. Several expeditions call for you to select literature to use with the project. Use this as an opportunity to differentiate instruction, coordinate with other subject teachers on an interdisciplinary unit, or focus on subjects of interest to your class or area.

Given the scope of each expedition, advance preparation is critical to successful implementation. As you prepare materials for each expedition, consider the needs of your classroom. You may wish to print out the student pages as a packet to give in its entirety to students, rather than hand them out in the suggested order. This will streamline your preparation time, as well as allow students who complete activities ahead of time to move on to the next phase.

About Project-Based Learning

In *Real Learning, Real Work*[1], Adria Steinberg describes the qualities of powerful projects: the six *A*'s.

Authenticity
Students solve problems and questions that are meaningful and real. People outside school walls tackle the same challenges. What students create and do has value beyond school.

Academic Rigor
Students encounter challenging material and learn critical skills, knowledge, and habits of mind essential for success in one or more disciplines.

Applied Learning
Students put their knowledge and skills to work in hands-on ways, and learn how to organize and manage themselves along the way.

Active Exploration
Students go into the field. They investigate and communicate their discoveries.

[1]Steinberg, Adria. *Real Learning, Real Work (Transforming Teaching)*. New York, NY: Routledge, 1998.

Introduction

Adult Relationships

Students connect with adults with relevant expertise. They observe them, work with them, and get support and feedback.

Assessment

Students play an active role in defining their goals and assessing their progress. Adults around them give them ongoing and varied opportunities to demonstrate progress.

Project Format and Materials

Each project contains the following materials:

Teacher Pages

- **Introduction:** includes an overview of information on project learning goals, plus information on prior knowledge or experience needed by students, time and materials needed for the project, key vocabulary, suggested assessment, and team formation
- **Suggested Steps:** a day-by-day view of how to implement project activities
- **Project Management Tips and Notes:** suggestions for how to handle possible issues or information on project options and variations
- **Extension Activities:** suggested activities for extending the project or exploring related areas
- **Common Core State Standards Connection:** a list of standards your students will address through the project
  * Lettered standards that are marked with asterisks vary slightly by grade. The skills most prominently addressed are included in the standards section, listed on the teacher pages for each expedition. For the full text of each standard by grade, see the CCSS for ELA at www.corestandards.org.
- **Answer Key:** answers for Skill Check questions (Some answers may vary, and therefore, have been omitted from the answer keys.)

Student Pages

- **Expedition Overview:** a description of the project challenge, learning objectives, key vocabulary terms, materials needed, and Web resources students use for project activities
- **Before You Go:** lead-in activities designed to review fundamental skills or knowledge needed for the project
- **Off You Go:** activities that support the core project, including guidelines and instructions for final products or presentations
- **Expedition Tools:** handouts and worksheets associated with project activities
- **Check Yourself:** two assessment tools that students use to check skill development (practice problems or questions) and evaluate their project performance overall

Project Skills Chart

Projects always challenge students to flex more than one mental muscle at a time and integrate skills they often see dissected and covered in discrete units of study. Each project in this book has a core skill focus, but also gives students an opportunity to practice other skills. Use this chart as a reference to help you find the best project for your needs.

C = Core skill

X = Other skills covered (sometimes optional)

Project	Grammar/mechanics	Writing skills	Creative writing	Critical reading	Communication/public speaking	Visual presentation	American literature	Literary genres/responding to literature	Research skills
Making History	X	C	X	C			C	C	
The World Around You	X	C	C			C			X
Who, Me?	X	C					C		
College Sales		C		X		C		X	X
Taking a Stand	X	C		C	C	X			C
Your Quest	X	C		C	C	X			C
Finding Your Roots	X	C							
Class Ezine	C	C			C	C		C	
You're the Playwright			C		C		C	C	
The Great Debate		C			C			C	C

Project Assessment Rubric

English Language Arts Project Assessment Rubric

	% of grade	4 (Excellent)	3 (Good)	2 (Fair)	1 (Poor)
Knowledge and skills specific to the project		Defines all key vocabulary, with examples. Actively uses terms, methods, and skills and transfers them to other situations and contexts.	Defines majority of terms, with examples. Majority of skills or methods are applied correctly. Sometimes transfers them to other situations or contexts.	Definitions and explanations are confusing or incorrect. Some skills used correctly.	No evidence of knowledge or skill development. Few correct methods, few correct answers.
Research		Work shows high-quality research on topic or theme. Research is used consistently to support main claims or points. Sources are reputable and cited correctly.	Work reflects solid research. Research is used to support most main claims or points. Sources are reputable and cited correctly.	There is little evidence of research, or research is used inconsistently to support claims or points. Citations are incorrect or incomplete. Sources are questionable.	There is no evidence of research. No citations are provided.
Grammar, spelling, and punctuation		Excellent use of mechanics. Sentences are well constructed. Student reviews work methodically for errors.	Uses mechanics consistently. There is some variety in sentence construction. Student reviews work for errors.	Inconsistent control of mechanics. Student reviews work for errors.	There are serious errors. There is little or no attempt to check work.
Writing		Purpose or argument is focused, well presented, and insightful. Includes excellent supporting detail. Shows creativity.	Purpose is clear and presented in an organized, engaging way. Includes relevant supporting detail.	Purpose or argument is vague. Organization is weak or inconsistent.	Topic is unclear. There are few supporting details and little evidence of organization.
Critical reading/ responding to literature		Provides excellent summaries of main ideas and themes. Pays close attention to detail and context. Insightful understanding of the author's purpose or point of view.	Summarizes ideas and themes adequately. Pays attention to details and context. Good understanding of the author's purpose or point of view.	Can summarize action or characters but struggles to summarize ideas and themes. Some difficulty interpreting information or drawing conclusions.	Cannot summarize ideas or themes. There is little or no attention to detail or context. Contributes little or nothing to discussion.
Final product		Meets all criteria. Organization and information exceed expectations. Reflects excellent understanding of project content.	Meets all criteria. Organization and information presented clearly. Reflects good understanding of project content.	Meets most criteria. Some elements or components are missing.	Did not contribute; did not submit or missing major components.
Presentation		Completed within specific time. Evidence of preparation is obvious. Emphasizes most important information. All team members are involved.	Almost completed within time. Preparation evident. Covers majority of main points. Most team members involved.	Almost completed within time. Little preparation evident. Misses a number of important points. Not all team members involved.	Did not participate, no preparation, way under or over time, or information is confusing and disjointed.
Teamwork		Workload divided and shared equally by all members.	Most members, including student, contributed fair share.	Workloads varied considerably. Student did not contribute fair share.	Few members contributed. Student made little to no contribution.
Class participation		Contributed substantially.	Contributed fair share.	Contributed some.	Contributed very little.

Making History

Overview
Students explore the lives of teenagers in the late nineteenth and early twentieth centuries. They examine primary sources to understand how these documents provide a picture of life during that time period. Students create a journal of a day in their life in their community to be archived for historians in the future.

Time
Total time: 8 to 10 hours
- **Before You Go—Getting Acquainted with Characters, Settings, and Plot:** one class, pp. 11–13
- **Activity 1—What's in My Reading?** one class and 30 minutes of homework, pp. 14–18
- **Activity 2—It's in the Details:** one class and 20 minutes of homework, pp. 19–21
- **Activity 3—Recording My Life:** one class and 30 minutes of homework, pp. 22–23
- **Activity 4—For All Time:** three to four classes, pp. 24–29
- **Check Yourself! Skill Check** and **Self-Assessment and Reflection** worksheets: 30 minutes of class time or homework, pp. 30–31

Materials
- notebook
- reading material (historical fiction excerpt or whole book)
- computer access (optional)

Skill Focus
- character
- setting
- descriptive and narrative writing skills
- editing

Prior Knowledge
- active reading
- writing process

Team Formation
- Students work individually, in small groups, and as a whole class.

Making History

Lingo to Learn—Terms to Know
- **biography:** a written account of another person's life
- **character:** the identity of an individual figure in a story
- **characterization:** the method a writer uses to develop a character
- **historical fiction:** a story that may not be true but is based on actual facts, places, a time period, or an event
- **narrative:** the telling of fictional or real events
- **plot:** the plan of the events in a story or the actions taken by the characters in a setting
- **setting:** the time and place of an action in a story

Suggested Steps
Preparation
- Review all the materials and activities for the expedition. Note printables that you'll need to copy.
- Select historical fiction or biographies for your students to read about children's lives from the 1860s to 1920s. You can choose whole books or short excerpts. The materials can be varied in order to match reading levels of your students. The time period can fluctuate; it is just important to provide a historical perspective.
- Students must complete their reading before starting these activities. The activities enable them to apply their understanding of character development and setting in literature. While students read, direct them to take notes on the main characters, describing the relationships between the characters and personality traits. Students should also take notes on the main plots, especially noting the settings.
- This expedition is in three steps:
  1. Students read the historical fiction or biography (completed before the beginning of the project).

  2. Students build a picture of the historical context from primary sources.

  3. Students write a journal entry for a recent event, expanding upon it to create a journal entry for a significant event that can be archived.

- It might be beneficial to enlist the support of a social studies teacher in the project.
- The project is best done in partnership with the local historical society. Consider inviting a speaker from the local historical society to your class. You can find information about historical societies in your state at the National Archives Web site at www.archives.gov/research/alic/reference/state-archives.html.

Making History

Day 1

1. Give an overview of the project. Explain that students will be developing a booklet of journal pages that represent what present life is like. These personal accounts can then be archived, perhaps with help from the local historical society. In the future, individuals can use them as background for writing biographies or historical fiction.

2. If possible, have a representative from a local historical society speak to the class about life at the turn of the century and the role of archived records from individuals.

3. As a whole class, complete and discuss **Before You Go: Getting Acquainted with Characters, Settings, and Plot** (p. 11), along with **Expedition Tool:** *Times* **Excerpt** (pp. 12–13).

Day 2

1. Distribute **Activity 1: What's in My Reading?** (pp. 14–15) and **Expedition Tool: Charting Character, Setting, and Plot** (pp. 16–18).

2. Read out loud the first section of the reading material you selected for the lower-level readers in the class. Have students reading that selection follow the text in their books. The other students can listen. It is best if you stop periodically, and then go back and review each section while pointing out what might be appropriate to place in the Expedition Tool.

3. Conduct a whole-class discussion, summarizing what students have learned.

4. Pair students by those who have read the same materials. Assign pairs to complete the Expedition Tool for their reading.

Homework

Students should complete the Expedition Tool.

Day 3

1. Pair students based on common readings. Facilitate a review of the completed Expedition Tool assignment.

2. Invite pairs to share their favorite part of their reading with the whole class, describing why it was chosen.

3. Compile all responses to create a master list of characteristics of good writing. Identify how these qualities relate to character, setting, or plot development.

4. Distribute **Activity 2: It's in the Details** (p. 19) and **Expedition Tool: Part of the Story** (pp. 20–21). Once students have rated the selections, tally the votes.

Making History

5. Discuss the selections with students, having voters express why they liked a particular selection. Add to the master list of the characteristics of good writing.

6. Have students work in pairs to identify how the selections with the fewest votes could have been improved. Ask students to discuss their ideas with the whole class.

Homework

Have students revise the selection with the fewest number of votes.

Day 4

1. Review the definition of historical fiction. Invite students to reflect on their reading and cite examples of text that is historically accurate and examples of text that is fictional. (For example, the story might be about slavery, which was an historical event, but the specific characters and their actions were fictional.)

2. Define and discuss the term *primary source.* Explain that a primary source is an actual item or document from an individual's everyday life. Examples include journals, letters, bills, and so forth.

3. Read aloud a primary source journal entry to the class. Choose a document from the pertinent era and geographic region (such as New England or the Midwest). Discuss the difference between the primary source and the literature students are reading. Note how authors use primary sources as research for developing their biographies of historical figures and historical fiction.

4. Use an overhead projector and transparencies, or a computer and projector to show some historical photographs of the appropriate era.

5. Identify the differences in settings, both geographically and in the scenes.

6. As each image is shown, invite students to describe what they see. Encourage them to enrich their descriptions by describing the actions, objects, or expressions in detail.

7. Distribute **Activity 3: Recording My Life** (p. 22) and **Expedition Tool: My Journal** (p. 23).

8. Explain that journaling is a type of narrative or story-telling. It is a written account of a person's activities. Connect it with familiar forms such as diaries, blogs, hunting or exercise/training logs, letters, photo journals, or lyrics.

Homework

Have students complete the Expedition Tool. They will write a journal entry that describes an event they did over the past weekend using what they have learned about quality descriptions.

Making History

Day 5

1. Give students time to share their journal entries. Encourage them to give one another positive feedback on their work and to identify the qualities of good writing.

2. Distribute **Activity 4: For All Time** (pp. 24–25) and **Expedition Tool: A Day in the Life of . . .** (pp. 26–29).

3. Explain that students are to draft another journal entry to be archived. Use the primary source documents from the turn of the century as models. Remind students that their journal entries will be read in the future to provide an understanding of what life was like during this time period.

4. Model the planning process with the Expedition Tool.

5. Have students work in pairs, taking turns to describe their own personal idea or event they want to convey to the reader. Pairs are to provide feedback to each other, revise their ideas, and then share with the whole class.

6. Select one idea from those presented by the class. Use this as an example to show the next steps in the writing process. Have students work with their partners to identify some supporting details. Have students share these, and select a few.

7. Student pairs should then add details of both setting and characters to the supporting details, indicating where these might appear in the story. Discuss as a class.

Homework

Have students continue to follow the steps in the writing process and arrange the supporting details for the example in a logical sequence. Students can review their notes from class to check that the original idea and the supporting details still match. If necessary, they should revise their work.

Day 6 (Narrative Writing)

1. Have students share their homework with a partner.

2. Give students time to work independently on authoring their own journal narrative. If students have difficulty selecting an idea, have them brainstorm a list of events that they have participated in during the past year—birthdays, sports, class projects, and so forth.

3. Once students have created an outline, have them share it with a partner for feedback and revise as needed.

4. Provide time for students to begin writing. Students can review their notes on qualities of good writing. Remind them that their journals will be read by students 30, 50, or 100 years in the future who may not know anything about the culture that students are describing.

Making History

5. Facilitate a one-to-one writer's conference with each student to support his or her planning and writing.

6. As students finish their writing, have them use the Writing Checklist on the **Check Yourself! Self-Assessment and Reflection** worksheet (p. 31). Have them revise their work as necessary.

Homework
Students should continue with their writing.

Day 7 (Revision and completion)

1. Direct students to share their narrative with a partner. Partners should pay particular attention to the amount of detail. Have them use their notes on the qualities of good writing from earlier classes to assess the text. Have the author revise it as necessary.

2. Once a revision is completed, students should find another partner to proof the writing, checking it for grammar, spelling, and punctuation.

3. When final papers are turned in, compile them into a booklet.

4. If possible, present the booklet to the local historical society.

Final Day

1. Have students complete the **Check Yourself! Skill Check** questions (p. 30).

2. Check and review answers.

3. Have students complete the **Check Yourself! Self-Assessment and Reflection** worksheet (p. 31) and submit it (optional).

Project Management Tips and Notes

- When selecting the readings for students, choose ones that focus on history from your geographic region.
- Contact your local or regional historical society well before the start of the project. They might be able to assist you in finding readings, images, and primary source documents from their collections.
- The writing assignment can be supported by obtaining images of children during the selected time period from the Library of Congress Prints & Photographs Online Catalog (http://www.loc.gov/pictures/). A search under "children playing 1860–1920" will result in a wide variety of images from around the country that can be downloaded and printed. Make sure to select "Match any words" from the advanced search options. You may also be able to search for images of your particular state or region.

Making History

- Create a word wall with the terms used throughout the project. This allows students a quick reference point for their vocabulary when discussing the materials. Students can also keep a descriptive writing journal in which they write adjectives and adverbs that are new to them, as well as notes on techniques for adding descriptions.
- Doing a quickwrite in the first 5 minutes of each class in which students respond to a prompt with a description will help students become more fluid in their writing.
- When students share their writing, the class can build a stronger understanding of quality work. It is also a good opportunity to focus on applications of recently studied rules in grammar, punctuation, or spelling.

Suggested Assessment

Use the Project Assessment Rubric or the following point system:

Team and class participation	10 points
Before You Go	10 points
Activity 1	10 points
Activity 2	10 points
Activity 3	10 points
Activity 4	45 points
Self-Assessment and Reflection	5 points

Extension Activities

- Students can illustrate their journals.
- Students can add more historical details to what they have already written.
- Students can extend their journal entry to a short story.

Common Core State Standards Connection

Reading—Literature: Craft and Structure

RL.6.5. Analyze how a particular sentence, chapter, scene, or stanza fits into the overall structure of a text and contributes to the development of the theme, setting, or plot.

Reading—Literature: Key Ideas and Details

RL.8.2. Determine a theme or central idea of a text and analyze its development over the course of the text, including its relationship to the characters, setting, and plot….

RL.7.3. Analyze how particular elements of a story or drama interact (e.g., how setting shapes the characters or plot).

Making History

Reading—Literature: Integration of Knowledge and Ideas

RL.7.9. Compare and contrast a fictional portrayal of a time, place, or character and a historical account of the same period as a means of understanding how authors of fiction use or alter history.

Writing: Text Types and Purposes

W.6.3, W.7.3, W.8.3. Write narratives to develop real or imagined experiences or events using effective technique, relevant descriptive details, and well-structured event sequences.

    a. Engage and orient the reader by establishing a context and point of view and introducing a narrator and/or characters; organize an event sequence that unfolds naturally and logically.*

    b. Use narrative techniques, such as … description, to develop experiences, events, and/or characters.*

    d. Use precise words and phrases, relevant descriptive details, and sensory language to convey experiences and events.*

Writing: Production and Distribution of Writing

W.6.5. With some guidance and support from peers and adults, develop and strengthen writing as needed by planning, revising, editing, rewriting, or trying a new approach.

Language: Conventions of Standard English

L.6.1, L.7.1, L.8.1. Demonstrate command of the conventions of standard English grammar and usage when writing or speaking.

L.6.2b, L.7.2b, L.8.2c. Spell correctly.

Language: Knowledge of Language

L.6.3. L.7.3, L.8.3. Use knowledge of language and its conventions when writing, speaking, reading, or listening.

Answer Key

Check Yourself! Skill Check

    1. A plot is the series of events in a book or story.

    2. A character is one of the individuals described in a story.

    3. Setting is the time and location in which a story takes place.

    4. An author can increase the descriptions of the setting, involve the characters in conversation, or include an item or thoughts with which the reader can identify.

    5. Historical fiction is a story that has elements of factual information, such as a real place, time, or person. It properly reflects what is known about that time period by historians. However, the characters and the events do not have to be true. They can be fictional.

Making History

Expedition Overview

Challenge

Have you ever wanted to be a time-traveler? Have you ever wanted to see the future or investigate the past? Would you like to leave a record of who you are for everyone in the future to read? Many individuals have written journals of their lives that allow us to see what life was like during the historic period in which they lived. Now you will create a journal entry that will be kept for future time-travelers to discover.

Objectives

- To understand how an author reveals and develops character
- To strengthen your narrative and descriptive writing skills

Project Activities

Before You Go

- Getting Acquainted with Characters, Settings, and Plot

Off You Go

- Activity 1: What's in My Reading?
- Activity 2: It's in the Details
- Activity 3: Recording My Life
- Activity 4: For All Time

Expedition Tools

- *Times* Excerpt
- Charting Character, Setting, and Plot
- Part of the Story
- My Journal
- A Day in the Life of . . .

Other Materials Needed

- notebook
- reading material (provided by your teacher)

Lingo to Learn—Terms to Know

- biography
- character
- historical fiction
- characterization
- narrative
- plot
- setting

Making History

Expedition Overview

Helpful Web Resources

- escrapbooking—E-scraps: Autobiography, Personal Accounts, & Travel Narratives
  http://escrapbooking.com/escraps/autobiography/index.htm
- Federal Resources for Educational Excellence
  http://free.ed.gov/index.cfm
- Google News Archive Search
  http://news.google.com/archivesearch?ned=us
- The Library of Congress—American Memory Timeline
  www.loc.gov/teachers/classroommaterials/presentationsandactivities/presentations/timeline/
- The Library of Congress—American Memory: Voices from the Days of Slavery
  http://memory.loc.gov/ammem/collections/voices/index.html
- The Library of Congress Prints & Photographs Online Catalog
  http://www.loc.gov/pictures/

Making History

Before You Go

Getting Acquainted with Characters, Settings, and Plot

Goal:	To understand characters, settings, and narratives as literary tools
Materials:	notebook, pen or computer
Tool:	*Times* Excerpt

An important part of creating a story is deciding on the setting. The setting is the time and place of an action in a story. If the story isn't true but it includes real people, places, or events, the story might be historical fiction. If a story is about an actual person who lived at an earlier time, it is a historical biography.

Characters are the individuals about whom stories are told. When writing a story, an author might describe personality traits of a character. For instance, a character could be humorous, angry, or moody. Authors will also create a physical description of the character so the reader can imagine the character's appearance. An author creates the character by showing how the individual reacts to various situations in the story.

The plan of the events in a story or the actions taken by the characters in a setting are pieced together into a plot. Sometimes a story can have more than one plot. It can move between groups of characters that are doing different things at the same time. For instance, a group of students could be studying at school—this is a plot. However, some of those students might be in an English class doing one set of things, while others could be in a math class doing another set of activities. These are the subplots to the main story.

When you read a story, imagine that you are trying to follow the clues to solve a mystery. You must first find out who is involved—the characters. Next, you find out where each character is located—the setting. Finally, you find out what they were doing—the plot.

Making History

Expedition Tool

Directions

Read the excerpt contained in the *Times* **Excerpt Expedition Tool.** Then answer the questions below.

1. Who are the main characters? Describe their personalities.

2. Where are the characters? Describe the setting in which the excerpt takes place.

3. What are the characters doing? Describe the major activities that occur.

Making History

Expedition Tool

Times Excerpt

Three Dying Foes Made Friends

(Adapted from an article in *The Hartford Courant*, Jan. 14, 1915.)

To the Editor of The Courant:

I have read nothing more tender and moving than the letter found by a Red Cross agent at the side of a dead officer and forwarded to the person to whom it was addressed. The writer was a French cavalry officer engaged to a young American girl in Paris. It was written as he lay dying from wounds received in battle. Let it speak for itself.   *E.P.P.*

THERE are two other men lying near me. I do not think there is much hope for them either. One is an officer of a Scottish regiment and the other a German private. They were wounded after me, and when I came to, I found them bending over me, giving me first aid.

The Britisher was pouring water down my throat from his flask, while the German was trying to stop the bleeding of my wound. The Highlander had one of his legs shattered, and the German had several pieces of shrapnel buried in his side.

In spite of their own sufferings, they were trying to help me. When I was fully conscious, the German gave us a morphine injection and took one himself. His medical corps had provided him with the injection and the needle.

After the injection, feeling wonderfully at ease, we spoke of the lives we had lived before the war. We all spoke English, and we talked of the women we had left at home. Both the German and the Britisher had only been married a year. . . .

I wondered, and I supposed the others did too, why we had fought each other in this war. I looked at the Britisher, who was falling asleep, exhausted. In spite of his drawn face and mud-stained uniform, he looked the picture of freedom. Then I thought of the flag of France and all that France had done for liberty in fighting this war. Then I watched the German they had fought against, who had ceased to speak. He had taken a Prayer Book from his knapsack and was trying to read a service for soldiers wounded in battle.

And . . . while I watched him, I realized what we were fighting for. . . . He was dying in vain, while the Britisher and myself, by our deaths, would probably contribute something toward the cause of civilization and peace.

(The letter ends with a reference to the failing light and the roar of guns.)

Adapted from *The New York Times. Current History—A Monthly Magazine: The European War, March, 1915.*

Making History

Off You Go

Activity 1: What's in My Reading?

Goal:	To apply understanding of character, setting, and plot as literary components to your recent readings
Materials:	notebook, pen or computer
Tool:	Charting Character, Setting, and Plot

Directions

You have recently completed a reading that describes life in America at the turn of the twentieth century. During your reading, you should have taken notes on the characters, settings, and plot described. Use your notes to complete the charts in the **Charting Character, Setting, and Plot Expedition Tool** according to the instructions below.

1. In the first column of the **Main Characters** chart, list the names of the three to five key characters in the story you read. These characters are discussed throughout most of your reading.

2. In the second column, write a physical description of each character (age, gender, hair color, height, and so forth).

3. In the third column, describe the personality of the character (kind, thoughtful, mean, humorous, etc.).

4. In the fourth column, describe any relationships to the other main characters (son, brother, husband, and so forth).

5. In the first column of the **Main Settings** chart, identify the main locations in which the story occurs. This could be a farm where the main character lives. Or it could be a wagon train crossing the country.

6. In the second column, identify when the characters are in that setting. This could be a year, or it could be the age of a character.

7. In the third column, write a physical description of each setting. This could include the location being a woodland, mountain, or prairie. It could be a town with wide unpaved streets, a few stores, and a hotel, or it could be a tepee, a log cabin, or an urban two-story home.

(continued)

Making History

Off You Go

8. Fill out the chart **The Main Plot.** Beginning with the first box, describe the character's first actions in the story. This could be an action such as moving from a town to a farm. Or it could be a family gathering at home before a character goes off to war.

9. Draw an arrow from that action (for example, family gathering) to another box, and describe the next action (character goes off to war).

10. If the story separates into two storylines, perhaps one for each character, draw an arrow from the first box (family gathering) to another box. Indicate the action (for instance, the sister takes over farming the fields).

11. Continue until you have diagrammed all the main actions in the story plot.

Making History

Expedition Tool

Charting Character, Setting, and Plot

Main Characters

Character name	Physical description	Personality	Relationship to others

Making History

Expedition Tool

Charting Character, Setting, and Plot

Main Settings

Location	Time period	Description

Making History

Expedition Tool

Charting Character, Setting, and Plot

The Main Plot

Making History

Off You Go

Activity 2: It's in the Details

Goal:	To learn how descriptive details enhance writing
Materials:	pen or computer
Tool:	Part of the Story

Directions

1. Read the selections in the **Part of the Story Expedition Tool.**

2. Decide which selection you like the most. Number the selections from your favorite (number 1) to your least favorite (number 4).

3. Write three reasons why you like your first and second favorite selections. Be prepared to share your ideas with the class.

_____

_____

_____

_____

_____

_____

_____

_____

_____

_____

_____

_____

_____

_____

_____

_____

_____

Making History

Expedition Tool

Part of the Story

1. The women's work there is chiefly the planting of sweet potatoes, taro and other things. They also weed the gardens; and in the afternoon, they get food from the gardens and firewood from the bush. They bring all of this home to the village. They also have to clear the undergrowth from newly cleared bush. The men's work is mainly planting yam, banana and sugar cane. Each one is planted in its season. The men must also cut down the big trees and make fences in order to make new gardens.

   Williamson, Robert W. *The Mafulu: Mountain People of British New Guinea*. London: Macmillan and Co., 1912.

   Your rating: _____

2. As she walked this morning in her garden, her dark eyes were troubled. She let her grey garments sweep the ground unheeded. She imagined she followed Prince Radiance, who had come for one brief hour into her dull life. She could only wonder whether she must be always lonely as she now was. She wondered whether she must always wish in vain for such happiness as his land could give. Up and down the alleys of the garden she went. For a long time no one came to disturb her. Eventually, a voice broke in upon her thoughts.

   Adapted from Crownfield, Gertrude. *The Shadow Witch*. New York: E.P. Dutton & Company, 1922.

   Your rating: _____

3. If you travel through the flat plains of Australia, you may hear a strange sound. Beginning softly, you hear a high, whirring noise. It slowly grows louder and louder. Eventually, it becomes a fluttering, windy roar. If you are a newcomer to the area, you may be very puzzled. If you have been in Australia before, you may recognize the bull-roarer. The sound is from the native populations celebrating their tribal mysteries. The roaring noise is made to warn all women to keep away.

   Adapted from Lang, Andrew. *Custom and Myth*. Longmans, Green and Co., 1884.

   Your rating: _____

(continued)

Making History

Expedition Tool

4. What can be more delightful than a day in the woods after a good snow! If you have a good friend or two along, and perhaps your dogs, you ought to be happier than a king is.

   A forest is a fine place at any time, but when the ground is well covered with snow with a hard crust—the woods seem to possess a peculiar charm. You can go anywhere then. In the summer, the thick undergrowth, intertwining vines, and heavy lower branches, make it difficult to see into the dark forest. But in the winter all is open. Even the low, wet places are frozen and are easy to explore.

   Adapted from Stockton, Frank R. *Round-about Rambles in Lands of Fact and Fancy.* New York: Charles Scribner's Sons, 1910.

   Your rating: _____

Making History

Off You Go

Activity 3: Recording My Life

Goal:	To create an interesting journal entry
Materials:	notebook, pen or computer
Tool:	My Journal

Directions

1. Make a plan to write a journal entry that describes an activity that you did last weekend.

2. Think about the ways you learned about to make writing interesting. These might include the following:

   • adding adjectives and descriptive details to increase a reader's ability to picture a scene

   • using items in your descriptions a reader can personally identify with

   • describing the setting in which an activity is done

   • including interactions between characters that illustrate their personalities

3. With these in mind, describe the activity. Use the **My Journal Expedition Tool** to record your journal entry.

4. Write at least a page describing the activity. Use your own paper if you need more space. Be sure to introduce and describe the setting and all the individuals involved. If you have photographs of the event, you can use those to help add detail.

Making History

Expedition Tool

My Journal

Date: _____

_____

_____

_____

_____

_____

_____

_____

_____

_____

_____

_____

_____

_____

_____

_____

_____

_____

_____

_____

_____

_____

_____

Making History

Off You Go

Activity 4: For All Time

Goal:	To use character, setting, and plot to create an interesting journal entry to be archived
Materials:	notebook, pen or computer
Tool:	A Day in the Life of . . .

Directions

Organizing Your Journal

1. Using the **A Day in the Life of . . . Expedition Tool,** write a few sentences describing the event you will write about in your journal entry. This could be as general as "We celebrated my birthday at my grandmother's house. My mother's whole family was there."

2. Under **Supporting Details,** write at least three details about the event. This gives more detail to the plot and can create subplots. These can be such things as conversations between individuals or specific activities.

3. Number your supporting details in the order in which you will write about them.

4. Under **Individuals Involved**, list the characters that will be included in the story. You can create other names for people if you do not want readers to be able to identify them. Show where in the story people will be introduced by also listing them under the proper supporting detail.

5. After each person's name, note what he or she will be doing and write one or two physical characteristics of the person.

6. Next, describe the setting(s) for the activity. Describe each location so that a reader can clearly imagine it. Your description should include the following:

   • where the story takes place geographically (such as the town and state)

   • when the story takes place

   • a description of the surrounding landscape (such as downtown or farmland)

   • specifics about the buildings and rooms if appropriate

7. Decide when you will introduce the descriptions of the settings. List these under the supporting details.

(continued)

Making History

Off You Go

Writing Your Journal

1. After you have organized your ideas, write a draft of your journal entry on a separate sheet of paper. Be sure to include the date of the event.

2. Use the Writing Checklist in the **Check Yourself! Self-Assessment and Reflection** sheet to review your draft. Make any revisions needed.

3. Once revised, share your work with a partner to get any suggestions. Proofread the journal. Make any necessary revisions in grammar, punctuation, or spelling.

4. Create a final draft.

Making History

Expedition Tool

A Day in the Life of . . .

Writing Focus (Plot)

Describe the event.

_____

_____

_____

_____

_____

_____

Supporting Details

List at least three specific scenes you might describe.

1. Summary: _____

_____

_____

_____

_____

Characters: _____

_____

Setting: _____

_____

_____

_____

_____

(continued)

Making History

Expedition Tool

2. Summary: _____

_____

_____

_____

_____

Characters: _____

_____

Setting: _____

_____

_____

_____

3. Summary: _____

_____

_____

_____

_____

Characters: _____

_____

Setting: _____

_____

_____

_____

(*continued*)

Making History

Expedition Tool

Individuals Involved

1. Name: _____

   Action: _____

   _____

   _____

   _____

   _____

   Characteristics: _____

   _____

   _____

   _____

2. Name: _____

   Action: _____

   _____

   _____

   _____

   _____

   Characteristics: _____

   _____

   _____

   _____

(continued)

Making History

Expedition Tool

3. Name: _____

   Action: _____

   _____

   _____

   _____

   _____

   Characteristics: _____

   _____

   _____

   _____

   _____

Setting

   State: _____

   Town: _____

   Date: _____

   Landscape: _____

   _____

   _____

   _____

   _____

   Buildings: _____

   _____

   _____

   _____

Making History

Check Yourself!

Skill Check

1. In literary terms, what is plot?

_____

_____

_____

_____

2. In literary terms, what is a character?

_____

_____

_____

_____

3. In literary terms, what is setting?

_____

_____

_____

_____

4. How can an author make his or her writing more interesting?

_____

_____

_____

_____

5. What is historical fiction?

_____

_____

_____

_____

Making History

Check Yourself!

Self-Assessment and Reflection

Writing Checklist

- ❑ My story has an interesting beginning.
- ❑ My story contains clear descriptions and adequate detail.
- ❑ My story allows the reader to connect the story to his or her own life.
- ❑ My story includes interactions between characters that show their personalities.

Reflection

1. What were the most challenging aspects of this project for you and why?

_____

_____

_____

_____

2. Which skills did this project help you develop?

_____

_____

_____

_____

3. If you did this project again, what might you do differently and why?

_____

_____

_____

_____

The World Around You

Overview

Students will create a one-page informational brochure encouraging middle-school students and their families to use the local parks in your area.

Time

Total time: 8 to 10 hours

- **Before You Go—Analyzing Print Media:** two classes and 30 minutes of homework, pp. 44–50
- **Activity 1—What's in the Park?** one class and 60 minutes of homework, pp. 51–55
- **Activity 2—Analyzing Descriptive Writing:** one class and 30 minutes of homework, pp. 56–59
- **Activity 3—Writing Haiku:** two classes and 20 minutes of homework, p. 60
- **Activity 4—Design a Brochure:** two classes and 30 minutes of homework, pp. 61–63
- **Check Yourself! Skill Check** and **Self-Assessment and Reflection** worksheets: 30 minutes of class time or homework, pp. 64–66

Materials

- notebook
- examples of flyers and information sheets
- magazines for clipping pictures or text
- colored paper
- scissors
- tape or glue stick
- rulers
- colored pencils
- sticky notes
- white printer paper (8½" by 11")
- camera (optional)
- sketchpad (optional)
- computer access
- printer

Skill Focus

- communication
- descriptive writing
- haiku

The World Around You

Prior Knowledge
- use of adjectives and adverbs
- creative writing using senses

Team Formation
- Students work in pairs, as individuals, and as a whole class.

Lingo to Learn—Terms to Know
- **descriptive writing:** writing that uses specific details about people, places, or events that appeal to a reader's senses
- **design elements:** the color, shape and movement, space, and texture of a product
- **haiku:** a form of poetry that is three lines with a total of 17 syllables
- **layout:** the way headlines, blocks of text, and images are displayed on a page
- **poetry:** an imaginative description of an experience put in language that creates a response through meaning, sound, and rhythm

Suggested Steps
Preparation
- Review all the materials and activities for the expedition. Note printables that you'll need to copy.
- It might be helpful to contact the local parks and recreation department to obtain maps and literature on parks students will be visiting. If possible, invite a member of their staff to class to present background information on local parks and the purpose of the department.
- Find multiple examples of different brochures and flyers. They should include some headlines, text, and images. Students will use them to evaluate the effectiveness of the brochures, including communications and creativity.
- Collect magazines for the students to clip samples out of. Students will look for samples of images and text (headlines) that they can use to design their brochures. You might want to contact an art teacher to assist in the project.

Day 1
1. Describe the project to students. Explain that they will design a one-page informational brochure about a local park that will appeal to middle-school students. Each brochure will include a descriptive writing, a haiku poem, headlines, and suggested images.

2. If possible, have a speaker from the parks and recreation department describe to the class the cultural and natural history preserved locally. He or she could provide information on some of the activities and programs that are available at the parks.

3. Discuss communications through print media. If students are not familiar with this term, explain that communications through media includes advertisements in periodicals, flyers, posters, and brochures.

4. Brainstorm how companies communicate with the public in print (flyers, brochures, newspapers, and magazines) and through electronics (television, radio, iPods, and the Internet).

5. Have students work in pairs to make a list of five ideas that have been communicated to them in the past few days through print media (such as the selling of a product or an idea).

6. Reconvene the class to share ideas as a group.

7. Distribute **Before You Go: Analyzing Print Media** (pp. 44–48) and **Expedition Tool: What Is the Message?** (pp. 49–50).

8. Using an overhead or a computer and projector, show students an example of a one-page flyer or brochure.

9. Have students work in pairs to identify what the message of the brochure is. Students should write their answer on the activity page.

10. Discuss students' ideas as a class.

11. Have pairs identify parts of the brochure and continue to complete the activity page.

12. Have students discuss their ideas as a class. Students might identify images (including photographs or drawings) and text (which varies in size and font, and can be categorized as headlines and body).

13. Connect use of these components of a brochure to students' past experiences. Students might have created projects that included working with variations in text (fonts and text size) or used illustrations to help explain an idea.

14. Direct pairs to match the parts of the brochure with the purposes of the designer explained in the Expedition Tool.

Homework

Students should complete **Before You Go: Analyzing Print Media** (pp. 44–48). Ask them to look at additional magazines or brochures to find layouts that they like. Using those examples, students should identify at least two ideas that could be used for the park brochure.

The World Around You

Day 2

1. Have students work in pairs to analyze a one-page brochure or flyer.

2. Invite pairs to share some of their ideas with the class.

3. Have students analyze the graphic design elements of the piece they brought for their homework using the **Before You Go: Analyzing Print Media** activity pages (pp. 44–48).

4. Invite student volunteers to present what they found to the whole class.

5. Distribute **Activity 1: What's in the Park?** (p. 51) and **Expedition Tool: Write a Description** (pp. 52–55). Explain the assignment. Tell students that once they identify a park they can easily visit, they can go with a partner. Students should complete their work independently. More than one student should go to each park. Students should go with an adult.

Homework

Students are to go to the park and complete the Expedition Tool. They are to write a brief description of the physical characteristics of the park (not more than 250 words). Remind students to identify key features such as a pond, field, forest, ball field, historic building, and so forth. Students are to add descriptive words for these features. They should also list any park activities such as walking, skateboarding, jogging, playing baseball, and so forth.

Day 3

1. Group students together who went to the same park.

2. Direct groups to share their descriptions with one another and identify which aspects of the park would be most important for the flyer.

3. Have the whole class discuss which characteristics of the park would be most appealing to middle-school students.

4. On **Expedition Tool: Write a Description** (pp. 52–55), have each student make a notation on the chart of physical features, noting which features the class felt were most important.

5. Distribute **Activity 2: Analyzing Descriptive Writing** (pp. 56–58) and **Expedition Tool: Good Detail Chart** (p. 59).

6. Assign the sample paragraph in Part 1. Have students read once for comprehension and a second time for analysis. Remind them to underline each description, circling the details.

7. In the Good Detail Chart, have students put the items described in the first column and the descriptive adjectives, adverbs, or phrases in the second column.

8. Discuss students' findings. Ask students to explain their reactions to the extra details and their ideas of why the author added the descriptions.

9. Assign the sample paragraph in Part 2 and have students complete the same analysis. Have them note unusual word associations such as *mice dancing* and *coyotes swearing*.

10. As a class, discuss why students think the author used particular word associations.

11. Give students time to read the next three sample paragraphs in Part 3 that all describe the same event. Students should choose which they liked best. Explain that they are to analyze how the paragraphs are different and explain why they liked their favorite.

12. Discuss student ideas.

Homework

Have students revise their brief descriptions of the park, this time addressing the style features they found in the sample readings.

Day 4

1. Have students work in pairs to share their revised writing and give feedback on what was appealing.

2. Distribute **Activity 3: Writing Haiku** (p. 60).

3. Have students read the description of haiku. Supply them with additional background on haiku if necessary.

4. Lead a choral read-aloud of the sample haiku.

5. Direct students to work in pairs to discuss what the poem means.

6. Analyze the poem's meaning with the whole class.

7. Review syllables, and discuss how many syllables are in each word in the haiku.

8. Review the form for haiku and guide students in determining if the poem is in the correct form.

9. Tell students to refer back to their notes about the activities that occur at the park. They are to select one of the activities and write a haiku about that activity. The poem will become part of their one-page brochure.

10. Choose any appropriate activity for the class to write a haiku about together.

The World Around You

11. After modeling, have students write a haiku on the chosen activity with a partner.

12. Invite volunteers to share haikus with the class.

13. Write each haiku on an overhead or the blackboard. Analyze the haiku form. Invite students to provide feedback on what they like or what changes they suggest.

14. Repeat several times to provide students with experience in seeing and hearing this type of poetry.

Homework

Have students work on their haikus if needed.

Day 5

1. Have a poetry fest. Divide the class into teams of three. Match each team with another team. Teams will work together, and each student will provide peer feedback to the members of the other team.

2. Give each student three index cards. Have students write the names of the three students from the other team on the cards.

3. Tell students that the peer feedback should indicate what they liked about the poem and make suggestions for improvement.

4. Set a "stage" for each student to read his or her haiku to the class. At the end of class, have the students exchange their peer comments.

Homework

Have students revise their haikus if needed.

Day 6

1. Distribute **Activity 4: Design a Brochure** (pp. 61–62) and **Expedition Tool: Sample Layout** (p. 63).

2. Explain that students are to use a pencil to make a 1-inch grid on a standard sheet of white paper.

3. Point out the text block samples in the Expedition Tool. Tell the class that the blocks represent the amount of space they have to write a description and haiku. The larger Text Sample Box block is about the size of their 200-word descriptive writing. The smaller block is the approximate size for a haiku with 16-point type.

The World Around You

4. Provide time for students to cut the blocks from the Expedition Tool or from another sheet of paper. Make sure that they create headlines (largest text size) for the name of the park. Students can cut out words and letters from magazines or type their headlines and print them out. Suggest that for sub-headlines, which are slightly smaller, students include park contact information.

5. Help students place the remaining text blocks on the grid. Students can also place colored blocks that are the size of images they want to include.

6. Remind students to be sure that they left 20 to 40 percent of the brochure as white space.

7. Allow students to revise their layout until they have the correct emphasis and movement across the page. Encourage them to use colored pencils to indicate any shading or word emphasis.

8. Have students check their design by reviewing the questions they answered in **Before You Go: Analyzing Print Media** (pp. 44–48).

9. Sign off on each design before students glue or tape the blocks in place.

Homework

Have students use a computer and word-processing program, or cut and paste a final version of their brochure with the correct text. Encourage students to find and use appropriate copyright-free images. Suggest that they can request to use an image from the parks and recreation department. If students can not find copyright-free images, remind students to document sources for copyrighted images they might use.

Day 7

1. If possible, invite the parks and recreation department staff to review the final products.

2. Have students display their brochures. If students visited more than one park, group sheets on the same park together.

3. When all the brochures are posted, pair students. Give each pair some sticky notes and have them follow the directions at the end of **Activity 4: Design a Brochure** (pp. 61–63).

4. Direct the pairs to review all the brochures. Instruct them to post positive, constructive feedback for each student designer.

5. Have students vote for first, second, and third most effective brochure for each park. You might wish to offer winning brochures to the parks and recreation department for use in their publicity.

The World Around You

Final Day

1. Have students complete the **Check Yourself! Skill Check** questions (p. 64).

2. Check and review answers.

3. Have students complete the **Check Yourself! Self-Assessment and Reflection** worksheet (pp. 65–66) and submit it (optional).

Project Management Tips and Notes

- Display examples of layouts and writing for students to refer to as the project progresses.
- If possible, team-teach with your school's art teacher to facilitate the project. He or she might be able to provide more examples on design elements. He or she might also be able to visit a class and give students feedback during their final design phase.
- To provide practice with descriptive writing, assign quickwrites. These are quick writing assignments in response to a prompt, often done in the first 5 minutes of a class. You could ask students to tell about an event the day before, describe a place they visited over the weekend, or give a sensory description of an item.
- Poetry is not easy for many students. There are forms of haiku that are not as rigid in the use of syllables. If students are having trouble with the form described, you may want to introduce more relaxed forms.

Suggested Assessment

Use the Project Assessment Rubric or the following point system:

Team and class participation	10 points
Before You Go	10 points
Activity 1	15 points
Activity 2	10 points
Activity 3	15 points
Activity 4	35 points
Self-Assessment and Reflection	5 points

The World Around You

Extension Activities

- Students can take their own pictures or make their own drawings for the information sheet.
- Students can create a tri-fold brochure using word-processing or graphic-design software.
- Students can do additional research on one aspect of the park and focus their brochure on that. For instance, if it is an historic park, students could research the event it commemorates. If it is a nature park, students could investigate the birds that use the park during different seasons.
- Students can create a podcast or video exploration of a park.

Common Core State Standards Connection

Reading—Informational Text: Key Ideas and Details

RI.6.2. Determine a central idea of a text and how it is conveyed through particular details….

RI.6.3. Analyze in detail how a key individual, event, or idea is introduced, illustrated, and elaborated in a text (e.g., through examples or anecdotes).

Reading—Informational Text: Craft and Structure

RI.6.5. Analyze how a particular sentence, paragraph, chapter, or section fits into the overall structure of a text and contributes to the development of the ideas.

RI.7.5. Analyze the structure an author uses to organize a text, including how the major sections contribute to the whole and to the development of the ideas.

RI.6.6. Determine an author's point of view or purpose in a text and explain how it is conveyed in the text.

Reading—Informational Text: Integration of Knowledge and Ideas

RI.6.7. Integrate information presented in different media or formats (e.g., visually, quantitatively) as well as in words to develop a coherent understanding of a topic or issue.

Writing: Text Types and Purposes

W.6.2, W.7.2, W.8.2. Write informative/explanatory texts to examine a topic and convey ideas, concepts, and information through the selection, organization, and analysis of relevant content.

   a. Introduce a topic; organize ideas, concepts, and information … include formatting (e.g., headings), graphics (e.g., charts, tables), and multimedia when useful to aiding comprehension.*

   b. Develop the topic with relevant, well-chosen facts, definitions, concrete details, quotations, or other information and examples.*

The World Around You

d. Use precise language and domain-specific vocabulary to inform about or explain the topic.

Writing: Production and Distribution of Writing

W.6.4, W.7.4, W.8.4. Produce clear and coherent writing in which the development, organization, and style are appropriate to task, purpose, and audience.

W.6.5. With some guidance and support from peers and adults, develop and strengthen writing as needed by planning, revising, editing, rewriting, or trying a new approach.

Writing: Research to Build and Present Knowledge

W.6.8. Gather relevant information from multiple print and digital sources; assess the credibility of each source; and quote or paraphrase the data and conclusions of others while avoiding plagiarism and providing basic bibliographic information for sources.

W.7.8, W.8.8. Gather relevant information from multiple print and digital sources, using search terms effectively; assess the credibility and accuracy of each source; and quote or paraphrase the data and conclusions of others while avoiding plagiarism and following a standard format for citation.

Answer Key

Check Yourself! Skill Check

1. A layout is the way headlines, blocks of text, and images are displayed on a page.

2. A graphic designer uses color, shape and movement, space, and texture to create a message along with the text.

3. Descriptive writing is writing that uses specific details about people, places, or events that appeal to a reader's senses.

4. By inviting a reader into a text, an author increases a reader's interest by providing clear, active descriptions that illustrate an emotion or the personality of a character.

5. A haiku usually has three lines with a total of 17 syllables. The haiku poem usually addresses an emotion evoked from a fleeting event, usually in nature.

The World Around You

Expedition Overview

Challenge

It's up to you to create some new publicity encouraging middle-school students and their families to use the local parks in your area. Your challenge is to design a one-page information sheet about a park that would appeal to middle-school students. Each information sheet should include a descriptive paragraph, a haiku poem, headlines, and suggested images.

Objectives

- To learn how to complete a graphic design
- To improve descriptive writing techniques
- To write engaging haiku poetry

Project Activities

Before You Go

- Analyzing Print Media

Off You Go

- Activity 1: What's in the Park?
- Activity 2: Analyzing Descriptive Writing
- Activity 3: Writing Haiku
- Activity 4: Design a Brochure

Expedition Tools

- What Is the Message?
- Write a Description
- Good Detail Chart
- Sample Layout

Other Materials Needed

- notebook
- examples of flyers and information sheets
- magazines for clipping pictures or text
- colored paper
- scissors
- tape or glue stick
- rulers
- colored pencils
- white paper (8½" by 11")

The World Around You

Expedition Overview

Lingo to Learn—Terms to Know

- descriptive writing
- design elements
- haiku
- layout
- poetry

Helpful Web Resources

- ABC's of the Writing Process
  www.angelfire.com/wi/writingprocess

- About.com—Desktop Publishing: Top 7 Page Composition Tips
  http://desktoppub.about.com/od/layout/tp/composition.htm

- Capital Community College Foundation—Guide to Grammar & Writing
  http://grammar.ccc.commnet.edu/grammar

- eNature.com—Field Guides
  www.enature.com/home

- Haiku for People
  www.toyomasu.com/haiku

- WritingDEN—Tips-O-Matic: Paragraphs
  www2.actden.com/writ_den/tips/paragrap/index.htm

The World Around You

Before You Go

Analyzing Print Media

Goal:	To learn about graphic design elements for print media in preparation for designing a one-page informational brochure
Materials:	flyer/brochure samples, pencil, magazines
Tool:	What Is the Message?

Directions

Read the **What Is the Message? Expedition Tool** on the elements of print media. Then work with a partner to analyze a one-page brochure or flyer provided by your teacher. With your partner, answer the questions below. Be prepared to share your ideas with your class. You will then use the questions to analyze a brochure or flyer you find on your own.

What Is the Message?

1. What are the designers of the brochure trying to tell you?

   _____

   _____

   _____

   _____

2. Does the designer want you to take action? If so, what?

   _____

   _____

   _____

   _____

(continued)

The World Around You

Before You Go

Parts of the Brochure

3. List the different parts of the brochure.

_____

_____

_____

_____

Levels of Information

4. Which parts of the brochure grab the reader's attention?

_____

_____

_____

_____

5. Which parts tell the story using few words?

_____

_____

_____

_____

6. Which parts give the reader more detail?

_____

_____

_____

_____

(continued)

The World Around You

Before You Go

7. Which parts ask the reader to take an action?

_____

_____

_____

_____

Graphic Design Elements

8. Are the colors used appealing? Explain.

_____

_____

_____

_____

9. Do the colors used match the feeling and message of the brochure? Explain.

_____

_____

_____

_____

10. Without reading the specific text or looking at the pictures, does your eye easily move in a Z pattern across and down the page? Do all the shapes help you move from one item to another? Explain.

_____

_____

_____

_____

(continued)

The World Around You

Before You Go

11. Are any blocks of text too large? Is a reader able to read the fine print?

_____

_____

_____

_____

12. Are the important words included in the headlines the right size? Would a hurried reader easily see them?

_____

_____

_____

_____

13. Does any block of text, image, or color make the eye move back up the page, stopping the reader from reading the entire message? Does any part of the design stop your eye?

_____

_____

_____

_____

14. Does the font selected match the message? (For example, a font named "Party Time" might not be appropriate for a brochure on health care.)

_____

_____

_____

_____

(continued)

The World Around You

Before You Go

15. Is the font easy to read in all the sizes used?

_____

_____

_____

_____

16. Do all the fonts used on the page complement one another? Do they allow the reader to easily find the most important information?

_____

_____

_____

_____

17. Is there enough white space in this flyer? Is it too packed with information or images?

_____

_____

_____

_____

The World Around You

Expedition Tool

What Is the Message?

Graphic designers try to "talk" to readers through print media. They usually want to catch the reader's attention, tell a story, and have readers take some action after reading the material.

Parts of a Brochure

When graphic artists begin their design, they think about the parts of the brochure they will use to represent each part of what they want to say. This includes headlines, subheads, images, and blocks of text.

Levels of Information

Each part of the flyer will be used for at least one of the following three purposes, called levels of information:

- getting a reader's attention
- telling the reader a story in greater and greater detail
- getting the reader to take an action

Graphic Design Elements

Graphic designers specialize in using images and words to communicate ideas. They want their work to do the following:

- grab the reader's attention
- give the reader an immediate sense of the content
- pique curiosity so the reader is interested in reading more
- provide enough information to prompt the reader to take action

The actions could be things such as buying a product, joining an organization, or looking at a Web site to get more information.

When graphic artists create designs to communicate ideas, there are four design tools they use—color, shape and movement, texture, and space. Color should match the message. For instance, if the message is about the outdoors, a designer might use greens accented with natural colors from flowers. The colors should point out the important parts of the message. Color can be used to create a mood or feeling for the design.

(continued)

The World Around You

Expedition Tool

Each part of a design can be seen as a shape of the overall space it covers. For instance, paragraphs of text are seen as repeating squares or a large rectangle. A photograph is a block the size of the image. These shapes should help the reader move from one part of the flyer to another, often in a *Z* pattern. The eye starts in the upper left corner of the page, moves across the page, down the page, and then from left to right.

Text can be formatted into many different fonts through word processing. Each font has different characteristics that make it useful for different purposes. Some fonts are humorous, some are easy to read, and some are old-fashioned.

If all the space on a page is used, the page can become too busy and confusing to the eye. The audience will not be able to move easily through the design and quickly get the message. A good rule of thumb is to have 20 to 40 percent of a page be white space. Blank areas are part of the design.

The World Around You

Off You Go

Activity 1: What's in the Park?

Goal:	To write a description of a local park
Materials:	pencil, camera (optional), sketchpad (optional)
Tool:	Write a Description

Directions

1. Visit a nearby park according to your teacher's instructions.

2. Take notes and complete the **Write a Description Expedition Tool.** List all the main physical features of the park, such as a field, forest, pond, baseball field, and so forth. Use lots of details to describe what you see.

3. After your visit to the park, write a short description of the physical features of the park on a separate sheet of paper. Your description should be no more than 250 words. Remember that the purpose of the short description will be to encourage students and their families to come to the park. You will do another activity later in which you will write about one of the activities you can do at the park.

4. Create a title for the description that you can use as a headline. Make the headline attention-getting so it will entice a reader to read more.

The World Around You

Expedition Tool

Write a Description

Name of park: _____

Date visited: _____

Physical Features of the Park

Feature	Details

(chart continues on next page)

The World Around You

Expedition Tool

Physical Features of the Park *(continued)*

Feature	Details

The World Around You

Expedition Tool

Activities in the Park

Activity	Details

(*chart continues on next page*)

The World Around You

Expedition Tool

Activities in the Park *(continued)*

Activity	Details

The World Around You

Off You Go

Activity 2: Analyzing Descriptive Writing

Goal:	To develop skills in descriptive writing
Materials:	pencil or computer
Tool:	Good Detail Chart

Directions

Part 1: Adding Good Detail

Read the paragraph below. Then answer the questions that follow.

Fishing

He paused in his thinking and let the outside world come into his open mind. East edge of a small lake, midday, there would be small fish in the reeds and lily pads, sunfish and bluegills, good eating fish, and he'd have to catch some for his one hot meal a day. Sun high overhead, warm on his back but not hot the way it had been earlier in the week; no, hot but not muggy. The summer was drying out, getting ready for fall. Loon cry off to the left, not distress, not a baby lost to pike or musky; the babies would be big enough now to evade danger on their own, almost ready to fly, and would not have to ride on their mother's backs for safety as they did when they were first hatched out.

Paulsen, Gary. *Brian's Hunt.* New York: Random House, Inc., 2003.

1. Go back and reread the paragraph. This time underline all the things being described and circle the descriptors for each thing.

2. Fill out the **Good Detail Chart** in the **Expedition Tool.**

3. Why do you think the author wrote the description the way he did? Be prepared to discuss your ideas with the class.

_____

_____

_____

_____

(continued)

Expeditions in Your Classroom: English Language Arts, Grades 6–8 © Walch Education

The World Around You

Off You Go

Part 2: Adding Surprise Associations
Read the paragraph below. Then answer the questions that follow.

Coyotes and Mice
He had heard that yip before when he'd watched a coyote hunting mice by a huge old pine log. The log had holes beneath it from one side to the other and the mice could dance back and forth beneath the log through the holes, while the coyote had to run around the end, or jump over the top, and the mice simply scurried back and forth under it to avoid him. The coyote tried everything, hiding, waiting, digging a hole big enough for himself under the log so he could move back and forth, but nothing worked. After over an hour of trying to get at the mice, he finally stood on top of the log looking down one side, then the other, raised his head and looked right at Brian as if he'd known Brian was there the whole time, and gave an irritated, downright angry yip. It was, Brian felt, a kind of swearing.

Paulsen, Gary. *Brian's Hunt.* New York: Random House, Inc., 2003.

1. Go back and reread the paragraph. Circle any words or phrases that surprised you.

2. Did the author use any words in an unusual way? Explain. Be prepared to discuss your ideas with the class.

_____

_____

_____

_____

Part 3: Connecting to the Reader
Read the three paragraphs below. Then answer the questions that follow.

A. George took a bike ride down the street to the store. He was getting ready to go away on a business trip to New York. His son Jim and his wife Susan would soon be home to say goodbye.

B. George, a brown-haired and blue-eyed man, about six feet tall and muscular, rode his new bike down the street to the store. His young six-year-old son Jim and his wife Susan with her long, black hair would soon be back to their apartment to say goodbye.

(continued)

The World Around You

Off You Go

C. George hopped on his new bicycle just one more time before he had to leave. He wanted to get some exercise before the long car trip. Buying a bottle of water was a good excuse to get outside and forget about the presentation he had to make in New York. By the time he got back to their apartment, his wife Susan and son Jim would be running up the street to hug him as they returned from kindergarten. George smiled proudly, remembering Susan's comment that Jim was just like him. He thought of the last time he went on a trip. Susan's long black hair blew in the breeze as she waved goodbye and lifted Jim so he could see the car disappear. George hated to leave them again.

1. Go back and reread the paragraphs above. Which paragraph do you like best? Why? What makes the paragraph appealing?

_____

_____

_____

_____

2. Describe how the three paragraphs are different. Be sure to include how the author's technique differs.

_____

_____

_____

_____

3. Based on what you have learned, revise your description of the park according to your teacher's instructions.

The World Around You

Expedition Tool

Good Detail Chart

Item described	Descriptive words and phrases

The World Around You

Off You Go

Activity 3: Writing Haiku

> **Goal:** To develop skills in writing haiku
>
> **Materials:** pencil and notebook or computer

Directions

Haiku is a form of poetry that developed in Japan. It has three lines and a total of 17 syllables.

It often has 5 syllables in the first line, 7 syllables in the second line, and 5 syllables in the third line. Haiku typically captures a moment. It expresses an author's feeling. Haiku often has a word in it that represents the season in which it takes place. There is also usually a break between two thoughts.

Read the example below and answer the questions that follow.

Moonlight shines brightly (___ syllables)
Mirroring the silver pond (___ syllables)
Dawn silently springs (___ syllables)

1. Work with a partner to analyze the haiku. What do you think it means?

   _____

   _____

   _____

   _____

2. Mark off the syllables in the haiku. Write the number of syllables next to each line.

3. Refer back to your notes on the activities that occur at the park you visited. Select one of the activities and write a haiku based on that activity. The poem will become part of your one-page information sheet on the park. Be prepared to share your haiku with the class.

Activity: _____

My Haiku

_____ (___ syllables)

_____ (___ syllables)

_____ (___ syllables)

The World Around You

Off You Go

Activity 4: Design a Brochure

Goal:	To create a one-page layout for a brochure or flyer
Materials:	colored paper, computer and printer, clear tape or glue stick, scissors, printer paper, ruler, colored pencils, sticky notes
Tool:	Sample Layout

Directions

1. Get a standard sheet of white paper (8½" by 11"). In pencil, mark a 1-inch scale on each edge. Connect the marks across the paper to create a 1-inch-square grid.

2. Look at the text block samples in the **Sample Layout Expedition Tool.** Each larger block contains about 100 words. (The text is in Latin because many design programs use Latin for sample layouts.) This should be about the size of your descriptive writing about the park. The smaller block is the approximate size for a haiku with 16-point type.

3. Cut the blocks from the Expedition Tool or use another sheet of paper. Make the blocks the size and shape you want for the brochure text.

4. To make your headlines, cut out words from magazines, type and print words, or use the text block in the Expedition Tool. Place your headline blocks on your grid. You should have a headline that has the name of the park along with a smaller block that includes the address, phone number, and Web site. You should also have a headline for your description.

5. Next, place your text blocks on the grid.

6. Finally, cut out a block for the size of image(s) you want on the sheet.

7. Move the blocks until you feel you have the correct emphasis and movement across the parts of the design.

8. Add any color for emphasis.

9. Check your design. Refer to the questions you answered in **Before You Go: Analyzing Print Media.**

10. When the design is finalized, glue or tape the blocks in place. Write on each block what should be contained in the block. Make any notes about color to highlight the design.

11. Create a final version of your brochure.

(continued)

The World Around You

Off You Go

12. Display your brochure and conduct a peer review of other students' brochures according to your teacher's instructions. Remember to do the following:

- Make positive, constructive comments about each brochure, noting what you like about it.

- Use sticky notes to vote for your three favorite designs for each park (mark them with a 1, 2, or 3 to signify your first, second, and third favorite).

Expedition Tool

Sample Layout

Kings Center County Park

Moonlight shines brightly
Mirroring the silver pond
Dawn silently springs

Sample Text Block

Nibh essissecte commy nisit luptat, conum et, quismolorer sectet, vel er summoloreril dipsum dionulla facidui eugait la faciduismod eumsandit lut augait am ipit doloborper am, vel ea facinim autat lor se tat lor si tet volore consed mod dolore modo consequatet iureet, consequisi.

Cor in exer acip essim am, sustie velit lore faci estio conullandio od tem qui bla autpat. Equat atinibh eu feum iniscid uissim velit velestie molore magna facipit er sendio dolobor sequis nim zzrit alis ea faccums andionu msandignim dolorer ostrud te magna consed modit ut lum ea facilit, sim ero conullam, doloreet ad molorercil exero.

IMAGE HERE

Sample Text Block

Nibh essissecte commy nisit luptat, conum et, quismolorer sectet, vel er summoloreril dipsum dionulla facidui eugait la faciduismod eumsandit lut augait am ipit doloborper am, vel ea facinim autat lor se tat lor si tet volore consed mod dolore modo consequatet iureet, consequisi.

Cor in exer acip essim am, sustie velit lore faci estio conullandio od tem qui bla autpat. Equat atinibh eu feum iniscid uissim velit velestie molore magna facipit er sendio dolobor sequis nim zzrit alis ea faccums andionu msandignim dolorer ostrud te magna consed modit ut lum ea facilit, sim ero conullam, consecte doloreet ad molorercil exero.

IMAGE HERE

Kings Center County Park
3247 Kings Blvd.
Oshmagosh, DE xxxxx-xxxx
(xxx) xxx-xxxx
For More information visit our
Web site: www.xxxxxxxxx.gov

The World Around You

Check Yourself!

Skill Check

1. In communications, what is a layout?

   _____

   _____

   _____

   _____

2. In communications, what are design elements?

   _____

   _____

   _____

   _____

3. In literary terms, what is descriptive writing?

   _____

   _____

   _____

   _____

4. What is meant by inviting the reader into a story?

   _____

   _____

   _____

   _____

5. What is the haiku form, and what it is usually used to describe?

   _____

   _____

   _____

   _____

Expeditions in Your Classroom: English Language Arts, Grades 6–8   © Walch Education

The World Around You

Check Yourself!

Self-Assessment and Reflection

Before You Go

❑ I understand the parts of a one-page layout that contribute to getting a message to the reader.

❑ I can analyze a one-page layout and identify how the parts contribute to the purpose of the piece.

❑ I know what design elements are and can analyze how well they help communicate a message in a one-page layout.

Off You Go

❑ I can analyze how an author creates a mood in descriptive writing.

❑ I know some techniques for improving descriptive writing.

❑ I know the form of haiku poetry and can write it.

❑ I know how to create a one-page layout in order to communicate information.

Do You Know?

❑ I can define the Lingo to Learn vocabulary terms for this project and give an example of each.

❑ I completed the Skill Check questions and carefully reviewed questions I did not answer correctly.

Reflection

1. What were the most challenging aspects of this project for you and why?

_____

_____

_____

_____

(continued)

The World Around you

Check Yourself

2. Which skills did this project help you develop?

_____

_____

_____

_____

3. If you did this project again, what might you do differently and why?

_____

_____

_____

_____

Who, Me?

Overview

Students will investigate a career available in your local area. They will identify the skills and training needed to become employed in this field. They will write a cover letter to a local business to inquire about work. Together, the class will create a resource for other students seeking employment.

Time

Total time: 3 to 4 hours
- **Before You Go—Job Search:** one class and 20 minutes of homework, pp. 74–76
- **Activity 1—Writing a Cover Letter:** two classes and 40 minutes of homework, pp. 77–79
- **Check Yourself! Skill Check** and **Self-Assessment and Reflection** worksheets: 30 minutes of class time or homework, pp. 80–81

Materials
- notebook
- newspaper with classified ads
- computer with Internet access (optional)

Skill Focus
- writing for a purpose
- editing and revising writing
- business communication

Prior Knowledge
- basic grammar and mechanics
- peer editing

Team Formation
- Students work in pairs, as individuals, and as a whole class.

Lingo to Learn—Terms to Know
- **business correspondence:** letters to a business written in a formal style
- **job skills:** work habits and knowledge that are required to perform a job

Who, Me?

Suggested Steps

Preparation

- Review all the materials and activities for the expedition. Note printables that you'll need to copy.
- Contact your school's guidance office to determine their interest in a packet on writing inquiries to businesses for jobs. Collect information on career opportunities in the area.
- Gather samples of job inquiry letters.
- It might be helpful to contact human resources offices of local businesses to request a presentation on career opportunities.
- You might wish to ask parents to present information on their careers and preparation.

Day 1

1. Have students complete a quickwrite, a short 5-minute written response to the following question: What type of career would you like to have, and what will you have to know to do it well?

2. Have students discuss responses in pairs and as a whole class.

3. Distribute **Before You Go: Job Search** (pp. 74–76).

4. Have students respond to the questions in Part 1 and share their responses with a partner.

5. Invite students to share ideas with the whole class.

6. Have students complete Part 2 of the activity. If possible, have the guidance counselor, people from local businesses, and/or parents present information about careers and the training needed to succeed. Or have students do online research to find out about different career fields.

7. Have students look at classified ads in the newspaper or use the Internet to find job opportunities in your area. As a class, put together a list of job opportunities.

Homework

Students select one job available locally and list the job skills that are required for the work.

Who, Me?

Day 2

1. Have students share their selected job and list of skills with a partner.

2. Distribute **Activity 1: Writing a Cover Letter** (p. 77), along with **Expedition Tool: Cover Letter Guidelines** (p. 78) and **Expedition Tool: Sample Cover Letter** (p. 79).

3. Direct students to read the cover letter guidelines.

4. Go over the sample cover letter inquiring about employment. Discuss the parts of the letter and how the letter is organized.

5. Prompt students to analyze the style in which the letter is written (scientific, personal, descriptive, narrative, essay, formal, informal, and so forth).

6. Ask students to outline their own cover letter using the guidelines in the Expedition Tool. Have them turn in their outlines.

Homework

Have students write the rough draft of a cover letter inquiring about work. Students should write to the company of their choice and convey the skills they have for the job. Students should imagine they have completed all the training needed.

Day 3

1. Provide time for students to share their letters with a partner for peer review.

2. Have a one-to-one meeting with each student to review organization and style.

3. All students should revise their writing.

4. When revisions are completed, ask students to find another partner to proofread their letter.

5. Ask students to make final revisions.

6. As a class, create a list of important points to keep in mind when inquiring about a job.

7. Compile the important points and the sample letters to create a packet. The guidance department might wish to have the packet available for all students.

Final Day

1. Have students complete the **Check Yourself! Skill Check** questions (p. 80).

2. Check and review answers.

3. Have students complete the **Check Yourself! Self-Assessment and Reflection** worksheet (p. 81) and submit it (optional).

Who, Me?

Project Management Tips and Notes

- Students often have ideas about a career they would like, but do not understand the wide variety of skills they will need to be successful. Individuals speaking to the students about their jobs will help them identify skills required.
- Students sometimes have trouble understanding a formal voice required in business correspondence. If this is a problem, it is helpful to have both good and bad examples of letters. Review the good examples first, then look at the bad examples, and ask students what they would recommend correcting.

Suggested Assessment

Use the Project Assessment Rubric or the following point system:

Team and class participation	20 points
Student quickwrite	15 points
Before You Go	20 points
Activity 1	40 points
Self-Assessment and Reflection	5 points

Extension Activities

- Students can create a best-case résumé.
- Students can investigate a particular career and write more specifically about the training and studies they would require.
- Students could create a "Careers in Our Town" brochure or pamphlet for the guidance department.

Common Core State Standards Connection

Reading—Informational Text: Craft and Structure

RI.6.5. Analyze how a particular sentence, paragraph, chapter, or section fits into the overall structure of a text and contributes to the development of the ideas.

Writing: Text Types and Purposes

W.6.2, W.7.2, W.8.2. Write informative/explanatory texts to examine a topic and convey ideas, concepts, and information through the selection, organization, and analysis of relevant content.

a. Introduce a topic; organize ideas, concepts, and information, using strategies such as definition, [and] classification ... include formatting (e.g., headings), [and] graphics (e.g., charts, tables) ... when useful to aiding comprehension.*

Who, Me?

b. Develop the topic with relevant, well-chosen facts, definitions, concrete details, quotations, or other information and examples.*

d. Use precise language and domain-specific vocabulary to inform about or explain the topic.

e. Establish and maintain a formal style.

f. Provide a concluding statement or section that follows from the information or explanation presented.*

Writing: Research to Build and Present Knowledge

W.6.8. Gather relevant information from multiple print and digital sources....

W.7.8, W.8.8. Gather relevant information from multiple print and digital sources, using search terms effectively....

Answer Key

Check Yourself! Skill Check

1. Job skills are the abilities needed to complete tasks given to you by your employer. These job skills might include typing, working in sales, working with computer programs, diagnosing illness or mechanical problems, using good grammar and writing style, doing graphic design, and so forth.

2. Business letters should be well organized, clear and concise, and formal. A business letter should highlight the main points and suggest the next action.

3. The main steps of the writing process are organizing, writing a draft, reviewing and editing, revising, and proofing.

Who, Me?

Expedition Overview

Challenge

The job search is on! In this Expedition, you will investigate a career available in your local area. You will identify the skills and training needed to become employed in this field. Imagining that you have completed this training, you will write a letter to a business asking about possible employment. Finally, you will identify the important points to remember when writing a cover letter and create a resource for other students seeking employment.

Objectives

- To learn about the job skills required to be employed in your field of interest
- To write a letter to a business inquiring about employment opportunities

Project Activities

Before You Go

- Job Search

Off You Go

- Activity 1: Writing a Cover Letter

Expedition Tools

- Cover Letter Guidelines
- Sample Cover Letter

Other Materials Needed

- notebook
- newspaper with classified ads
- computer with Internet access (optional)

Lingo to Learn—Terms to Know

- business correspondence
- job skills

Who, Me?

Expedition Overview

Helpful Web Resources

- About.com (English as 2nd Language)—Business Letter Writing: Writing a Cover Letter when Applying for a Job
  http://esl.about.com/library/writing/blwrite_cover.htm

- About.com (English as 2nd Language)—Guide to Basic Business Letters
  http://esl.about.com/cs/onthejobenglish/a/a_basbletter.htm

- Career Planner.com—Job & Career Outlook
  www.careerplanner.com/Job-Outlook-Index.cfm

- George Mason University Writing Center—Writing Business Letters
  http://writingcenter.gmu.edu/resources-template.php?id=29

- QuintCareers.com—The Basics of a Job-Seeker: Dynamic Cover Letter
  www.quintcareers.com/cover_letter_basics.html

Who, Me?

Before You Go

Job Search

> **Goal:** To identify careers of interest and learn about the job skills required for different careers
>
> **Materials:** notebook, newspaper with classified ads, computer with Internet access (optional)

Directions

Part 1: My Career Path

1. What do you love to do in your free time? List three to five things.

   _____

   _____

   _____

   _____

   _____

   _____

2. What do you think are your natural skills? List three to five things that are easy for you to do.

   _____

   _____

   _____

   _____

   _____

   _____

(*continued*)

Who, Me?

Before You Go

3. What types of activities do you get excited about doing? List three to five activities.

_____

_____

_____

_____

_____

_____

4. What are your favorite subjects to read about?

_____

_____

_____

_____

5. What kind of place would you like to work at, and what would you like to do there? For instance, would you like to work outdoors? On computers? Would you like a fast-paced job? A slow-paced one? Write your ideas below.

_____

_____

_____

_____

6. Do you like to help people? If so, list two or three ways that you like to help others.

_____

_____

_____

_____

(continued)

Who, Me?

Before You Go

7. Reflect on your answer to these questions, and then revise your response to the following question: What type of career would you like to have, and what will you have to know to do it well?

_____

_____

_____

_____

_____

_____

_____

_____

_____

_____

Part 2: Career Options

1. If you are listening to presentations regarding various careers and the training needed to succeed in them, take notes on a separate sheet of paper.

2. Use the Internet or a newspaper to research different career opportunities according to your teacher's instructions. With your class, create a list of the different job opportunities available in your area.

_____

_____

_____

3. Select one job available locally and list the job skills that are required for the work.

_____

_____

_____

Expeditions in Your Classroom: English Language Arts, Grades 6–8 © Walch Education

Who, Me?

Off You Go

Activity 1: Writing a Cover Letter

Goal:	To learn how to write a cover letter inquiring about employment
Materials:	notebook
Tools:	Cover Letter Guidelines, Sample Cover Letter

Directions

1. Read **Expedition Tool: Cover Letter Guidelines** and **Expedition Tool: Sample Cover Letter.**

2. Analyze the parts of the sample cover letter.

3. Imagine that you are writing the company of your choice to inquire about possible work. (Assume that you have already completed all the training you need in order to be successful at the job.) In your cover letter, you should identify the most important skills you have acquired and explain why you would be a good candidate for a job at the business.

4. In the space below or on a separate sheet of paper, outline your cover letter using the information in the Expedition Tools.

5. Write a rough draft of your letter.

6. Have a partner peer-edit your letter.

7. Revise your letter as needed.

8. Have another partner proofread your letter. Make any corrections necessary to complete the final draft.

Cover Letter Outline

_____

_____

_____

_____

_____

_____

_____

Who, Me?

Expedition Tool

Cover Letter Guidelines

A cover letter should be written in a formal voice. The letter should be brief and clear.

- The letter should open with an attention-grabber that is directly tied to the inquiry. The first paragraph should have a clear statement on why you would make a good employee.
- The middle paragraph should describe the experiences you have had that will make you a good employee. If you have someone who can recommend or verify your work, you can mention that person's name in this paragraph.
- You should close with a paragraph that includes what your next step will be in contacting the employer.
- You should add a closing such as *Sincerely* or *Gratefully,* followed by your signature.
- If you are including a résumé or additional information, you would mention that in the final paragraph. You would write *encl: Résumé,* the abbreviation for *enclosure* followed by the title of the enclosure.

Now read **Expedition Tool: Sample Cover Letter** on the next page.

Who, Me?

Expedition Tool

Sample Cover Letter

Janet Knowles
14 River Road
Somewhere, ME 04237
jknowles@mymail.com
555-555-2972

| Your contact information |

March 17, 2012

| Date |

Belle Saunders
Human Resources Department
Best Gadgets
Simpson, ME 04238

| Recipient's address |

Dear Ms. Saunders:

| The salutation or greeting is best addressed to a specific individual. |

The Best Gadgets store has been one of my favorite places to explore since I was very young. I have focused my education on keeping up with all of the latest gadgets, and I write my own blog evaluating new gadgets as they are brought to market. I am confident I would be a wonderful employee at the Best Gadgets store.

| The opening paragraph quickly identifies why you are writing. It opens with a high-interest statement that gets the reader's attention. It has a confident statement on why you would make a good employee. |

There are a great number of gadgets that come on the market every week. Analyzing these products requires a sound understanding of science principles, a strong background in comparing items to similar products, and a good understanding of value for the cost. As you can read in my blog, www.janetgadgetblog.com, many individuals have found my reviews using this knowledge helpful.

| Explain what specific skills you have. If possible, identify someone else who has found your skills useful, such as another employer, a teacher, or a volunteer supervisor. |

During my schooling, I have also taken courses on marketing and business book-keeping. I have received a 3.4 grade average throughout my two years of technical school. I have also served as a lab technician in one of my electronics courses.

| Add any additional skills or background. |

I would like to come and speak with you about employment opportunities. I can be available any weekday morning or on Saturday. I can be reached at 555-555-2972 or via e-mail at jknowles@mymail.com. I look forward to hearing from you. Thank you for your time and consideration.

Sincerely,

Janet Knowles

| Closing Signature |

Janet Knowles

| Let the person know you're interested in meeting and how to get in touch with you. Thank the person for his or her time. |

Who, Me?

Check Yourself!

Skill Check

1. What are job skills? Give some examples.

   _____

   _____

   _____

   _____

   _____

2. What are some important characteristics of a cover letter to a business?

   _____

   _____

   _____

   _____

   _____

3. What are the main steps of the writing process?

   _____

   _____

   _____

   _____

   _____

Who, Me?

Check Yourself!

Self-Assessment and Reflection

Before You Go

- ❏ I understand the things I should consider when deciding on a career.
- ❏ I know about possible jobs in my area and the skills required to do those jobs.

Off You Go

- ❏ I know how to write a cover letter inquiring about employment.

Do You Know?

- ❏ I can define the Lingo to Learn vocabulary terms for this project and give an example of each.
- ❏ I completed the Skill Check questions and carefully reviewed questions I did not answer correctly.

Reflection

1. What were the most challenging aspects of this project for you and why?

   _____

   _____

   _____

2. Which skills did this project help you develop?

   _____

   _____

   _____

3. If you did this project again, what might you do differently and why?

   _____

   _____

   _____

College Sales

Overview
Students will compare colleges and their offerings, and then create a brochure to communicate about their ideal college.

Time
Total time: 6 to 8 hours
- **Before You Go—Product Identity:** one class, p. 92
- **Before You Go—College Interview:** 60 minutes of homework, pp. 93–95
- **Activity 1—Selection Criteria:** one class and 30 minutes of homework, pp. 96–98
- **Activity 2—College Brochure:** three classes and 90 minutes of homework (60 minutes plus 30 minutes), pp. 99–100
- **Check Yourself! Skill Check** and **Self-Assessment and Reflection** worksheets: 30 minutes of class time or homework, pp. 101–102

Materials
- notebook
- college brochures or catalogs
- computer with Internet access (optional)
- magazines for clipping pictures or text
- white or colored paper
- notebook paper
- scissors
- clear tape
- rulers
- sticky notes

Skill Focus
- using descriptive and narrative writing skills
- reviewing grammar and sentence structure
- analyzing writing for different audiences
- writing for a purpose
- editing and revising writing

Prior Knowledge
- basic grammar and mechanics
- peer editing

College Sales

Team Formation

- Students work in pairs, as individuals, and as a whole class.

Lingo to Learn—Terms to Know

- **layout:** the way headlines, blocks of text, and images are displayed on a page
- **marketing:** the technique used by manufacturers to make buyers aware of their products
- **product identity:** how manufacturers label and market a product
- **selection criteria:** qualities used when comparing items in order to make a decision

Suggested Steps

Preparation

- Review all the materials and activities for the expedition. Note printables that you'll need to copy.
- Collect sample brochures and promotional materials. Make overheads or bookmark Web sites in order to project some of the information to the whole class.
- Contact the guidance office to obtain literature on various colleges.
- If possible, have the guidance counselor visit the class and make a presentation on various types of colleges (such as liberal arts colleges, technical colleges, and community colleges) and their offerings.
- You might want to contact the admissions office of your state university system to determine if they have any interest in the final product as an indicator of what middle-school students find important when considering college. You can also ask what they find to be important qualities in the students they admit.

Day 1

1. Have students complete a quickwrite, a short 5-minute written response to the following prompt: What is marketing, and how does it influence your decision-making?

2. Discuss students' ideas. Be sure to discuss both positive and negative aspects of marketing. Come to a consensus on a definition of marketing.

3. Distribute **Before You Go: Product Identity** (p. 92) and **Before You Go: College Interview** (pp. 93–95).

4. Have students select one item they or their families buy. They should identify one quality of the item that is most frequently mentioned or seen in an advertisement.

College Sales

5. Explain that phrases and images are part of a product identity. See if students can come up with examples such as logos on clothing and shoes (Nike, for example).

6. Ask students if they saw the exact same pair of shoes but one pair had a Nike logo and one did not, which would they purchase? How much more would they pay? Why?

7. Discuss with students whether they think there is any marketing involved in the college admission process.

8. Describe the project to the class. Students will investigate colleges to understand how they differ, and identify what would be important to them when considering a college. They will create a product identity through a brochure that markets their ideal, but realistic, college.

Homework

Have students interview two adult members of their family or community using the questions in **Before You Go: College Interview** (pp. 93–95). They should record their answers on important qualities they would look for in a college or university.

Day 2

1. If possible, have the guidance counselor present an overview on colleges and universities, including the different things they offer. Have the counselor point out that students must also market themselves when applying to colleges. He or she could also provide a brief overview of what the admission process entails.

2. Distribute **Activity 1: Selection Criteria** (pp. 96–97) and **Expedition Tool: College Characteristics** (p. 98).

3. Ask students if they feel colleges have product identities.

4. Share the features that students identified in their interviews to be most important in selecting a college. Create a master list of features on the board or overhead.

5. Title the list *Selection Criteria*.

6. Explain that students will create their own selection criteria for a college and then create a marketing tool for their ideal college.

7. Project the brochures or Web sites of two or three schools, one at a time.

8. While students are reading the information, instruct them to take notes in the Expedition Tool on the features that each school promotes as most important or unique.

College Sales

9. Have students work in pairs to review some additional literature about colleges. These can be additional Web sites, brochures, catalogs, or compendiums that describe schools and their offerings.

10. Ask students to describe the style of writing in the college literature. Is it personal, scientific, narrative, or descriptive?

11. As a class, compare the list of selection criteria and the information each student recorded in the table of college characteristics. Identify any matches.

Homework

Students should make a list of six to eight features that they consider most important for a college to have.

Day 3

1. Provide time for students to share their list of important features with a partner. The partner can help determine if all the features are realistic items a college could have.

2. Distribute **Activity 2: College Brochure** (pp. 99–100).

3. Explain that students will make a tri-fold brochure. They will each take a sheet of plain white paper and fold it in thirds.

4. Walk students through the folding and formatting process. Students should open the sheet again and number each of the six panels (numbers 1 to 3 on the front and 4 to 6 on the back of the page). Students fold the paper first from the right to the center and then from the left to the center. Panel 6 should be on top. Students write *Cover* at the top of panel 6, *Text* at the top of panels 1 through 4, and *Back* at the top of panel 5.

5. Tell students that the task will be to create a layout on this tri-fold brochure for their ideal college. They will create a cover that has the name of the college and a slogan that identifies the most important feature. The name of their ideal college should be typed to fit within the columns, approximately 1.5 inches in width. Type size should be at least 18 points for the cover.

6. As homework, students can write one to two brief paragraphs about each of their six to eight most important features. These should be descriptive details about the features of the college. Review the qualities of descriptive writing.

7. Look for student paragraphs to be typed in 12-point font to fit in the columns, approximately 1.5 inches wide. If students want to add any headlines, they can add these as bold text or in a larger font.

Teacher Page

8. The back panel in a brochure should be used as a summary of the inside points. Have students make a bulleted list of their ideal college's important features. The list should be the correct width.

Homework

Have students work on their paragraphs describing college features for the inside of the brochure and the summary for the back panel of the brochure.

Day 4

1. Give students time to cut apart the paragraphs and headlines for their desired features. Using clear tape, students should place the text in the four panels (numbers 1 through 4). Have them leave space for potential illustrations or images. If they have trouble with placing the text, have them review some of the brochures on hand to get ideas.

2. Direct students to place their bulleted list on the back panel. Afterwards, have them cut out their ideal school's name and create their cover.

3. Let the students look through the available magazines to see if there are any images they would like to use. Have them place these on the brochure with clear tape.

4. Provide time for students to peer-review the brochures with a partner. Remind students to suggest ways to clarify or expand the text. Have them also proof the materials and suggest changes in grammar, spelling, or punctuation.

Homework

Students should revise their text if needed. Students should bring all their text printed in the appropriate width.

Day 5

1. Have students make a new tri-fold layout on a sheet of white or colored printer paper.

2. Give students time to create their layout with the revised text.

3. Create small groups of three to five students. Give each student a sticky note for the brochure.

4. Students should review one another's work and write a short comment on each sticky note saying what they liked about the brochure.

5. Let the authors read the comments.

College Sales

6. Have a quick roundabout in which each student has 1 minute to say what he or she learned from the project.

7. If desired, invite the guidance counselor to class to see the brochures and hear the students' comments. You could ask the counselor to speak about the importance of selecting a college and finding what is important to them as students. He or she could also discuss what is important to colleges when admitting students.

8. Read any response you have received from the admissions office at the state university system.

9. Collect brochures to share with the guidance office.

Final Day
1. Have students complete the **Check Yourself! Skill Check** questions (p. 101).

2. Check and review answers.

3. Have students complete the **Check Yourself! Self-Assessment and Reflection** worksheet (p. 102) and submit it (optional).

Project Management Tips and Notes
- Some students may not have thought a great deal about college. They might not have family members who have ever attended college. If possible, obtain some college information from the guidance counselor that students can take home to review.
- Students might have questions about college that they do not want to ask in front of the class. In the classes preceding the start of the project, ask students to write down three questions they have about college. Forward these to the guidance counselor so that he or she can answer them if a talk to the class is planned.
- It might be helpful to involve other staff members in this project. The guidance counselor could provide information about colleges. The technology teacher could help with creating the word processing documents and finding possible Web sites to visit. The librarian could help with information on colleges. The art teacher could assist when the students are creating the layouts for the brochure.

College Sales

Suggested Assessment

Use the Project Assessment Rubric or the following point system:

Team and class participation	10 points
Student quickwrite	10 points
Before You Go: Product Identity	10 points
Before You Go: College Interview	10 points
Activity 1	15 points
Activity 2	40 points
Self-Assessment and Reflection	5 points

Extension Activities

- Students can interview students in upper grades about their selection criteria for schools.
- Students could do a summary report on what colleges are most interested in when selecting students for admission.
- Students could create a product of their own and create a product identity, including a brochure.

Common Core State Standards Connection

Reading—Informational Text: Integration of Knowledge and Ideas

RI.6.7. Integrate information presented in different media or formats (e.g., visually, quantitatively) as well as in words to develop a coherent understanding of a topic or issue.

Writing: Text Types and Purposes

W.6.2, W.7.2, W.8.2. Write informative/explanatory texts to examine a topic and convey ideas, concepts, and information through the selection, organization, and analysis of relevant content.

a. Introduce a topic; organize ideas, concepts, and information … using strategies such as definition, [and] classification … include formatting (e.g., headings), [and] graphics (e.g., charts, tables) … when useful to aiding comprehension.*

b. Develop the topic with relevant, well-chosen facts, definitions, concrete details, quotations, or other information and examples.*

d. Use precise language and domain-specific vocabulary to inform about or explain the topic.

College Sales

f. Provide a concluding statement or section that follows from the information or explanation presented.*

Writing: Production and Distribution of Writing

W.6.4, W.7.4, W.8.4. Produce clear and coherent writing in which the development, organization, and style are appropriate to task, purpose, and audience.

Answer Key
Check Yourself! Skill Check

1. A layout is the way headlines, blocks of text, and images are displayed on a page.

2. Product identity is how manufacturers label a product. They use communication tools to point out unique characteristics that they know customers want. Marketing is the technique used by these manufacturers to make buyers aware of their products, mostly through advertising in different media.

3. Selection criteria are qualities that you decide to use when comparing items in order to make a decision.

4. Descriptive writing is writing that uses specific details about people, places, or events that appeal to a reader's senses.

5. Answers will vary.

College Sales

Expedition Overview

Challenge

Have you ever thought about how marketing affects what you do, what you buy, and even what college you might attend? In this Expedition, you will learn about marketing and how companies create product identities. You will review colleges and identify the strategies they have used to communicate the features of their programs. Finally, you will create a brochure that markets your ideal college.

Objectives

- To learn about the role of communications in marketing
- To investigate colleges and how they are marketed to students
- To learn to design and write a brochure to communicate the offerings of an ideal college

Project Activities

Before You Go

- Product Identity
- College Interview

Off You Go

- Activity 1: Selection Criteria
- Activity 2: College Brochure

Expedition Tools

- College Characteristics

Other Materials Needed

- notebook
- college brochures or catalogs
- computer with Internet access (optional)
- magazine for clipping pictures or text
- white or colored paper
- scissors
- clear tape
- ruler
- sticky notes

College Sales

Expedition Overview

Lingo to Learn—Terms to Know
- layout
- marketing
- product identity
- selection criteria

Helpful Web Resources
- 50States.com—Colleges and Universities
  www.50states.com/college
- Colleges.com—Undergrad Search
  www.colleges.com/admissions/undergraduate/index.html
- Google—Search under "college brochure"
  www.google.com
- Microsoft—Create a Theme-Related Brochure in Word
  www.microsoft.com/education/en-us/teachers/how-to/Pages/theme-related-brochure.aspx
- U.S. News & World Report—Best Colleges
  http://colleges.usnews.rankingsandreviews.com/best-colleges

College Sales

Before You Go

Product Identity

Goal:	To learn about product identity as a part of marketing
Materials:	notebook

Directions

When a manufacturer makes a product, it usually creates a product identity to go along with it. This is a set of phrases and images that always accompany the product. The words might identify the unique qualities of the product. Advertisers use words that attract the attention of the audience, or the people they are trying to sell the product to. Often these words are incorporated into songs or jingles. The purpose is to have the person buying the product recognize the product name or logo, feel it is what he or she wants, and purchase it. For example, you probably recognize Nike's logo and associate it with well-known sports stars.

1. Select one item you or your family uses. Identify one quality or feature of the item that is most often mentioned in ads for the product.

   _____

   _____

   _____

   _____

   _____

   _____

2. What are some phrases that are associated with the product's advertising? Write them below.

   _____

   _____

   _____

   _____

   _____

   _____

College Sales

Before You Go

College Interview

> **Goal:** To conduct an interview regarding important qualities to look for in a college or university
>
> **Materials:** notebook

Directions

Interview two adult members of your family or community using the questions below. Write their answers below or on a separate sheet of paper. Once you and your classmates have completed the interviews, you will compile a list of important qualities to look for in a college or university.

Interview Questions

1. Why do you think it is important to attend college or technical school?

   Interview Subject 1:

   _____

   _____

   _____

   _____

   _____

   _____

   Interview Subject 2:

   _____

   _____

   _____

   _____

   _____

   _____

(continued)

College Sales

Before You Go

2. When choosing a college, what do you think are the two most important qualities to look for in a college campus?

Interview Subject 1:

_____

_____

_____

_____

_____

Interview Subject 2:

_____

_____

_____

_____

_____

3. When choosing a college, what do you think are the two most important qualities to look for in the college academic program?

Interview Subject 1:

_____

_____

_____

_____

_____

(*continued*)

College Sales

Before You Go

Interview Subject 2:

_____

_____

_____

_____

_____

_____

4. When choosing a college, what do you think are the two most important non-academic opportunities that should be available?

Interview Subject 1:

_____

_____

_____

_____

_____

_____

Interview Subject 2:

_____

_____

_____

_____

_____

_____

College Sales

Off You Go

Activity 1: Selection Criteria

Goal:	To learn about colleges, the variety of programs they offer, and the selection criteria individuals use to select a college
Materials:	notebook, college brochures and catalogs, computer with Internet access (optional)
Tool:	College Characteristics

Directions

1. Look at available information on various colleges and technical schools. Or, visit college Web sites according to your teacher's instructions.

2. For each school, note any features that are promoted as most important or unique. These are characteristics that create college identity. Write these features in the table in the **College Characteristics Expedition Tool.**

3. Work with a partner to review additional information about colleges and add it to the table.

4. Notice the style of writing that is used for the college brochures and Web pages. Is it personal, scientific, narrative, or descriptive? Why do you think so?

   _____

   _____

   _____

   _____

   _____

5. Review the list of important qualities of colleges compiled by the class. Below, write a list of six to eight features that you consider most important for the college you want to attend.

   Feature 1: _____

   _____

   _____

(continued)

College Sales

Off You Go

Feature 2: _____

_____

_____

Feature 3: _____

_____

_____

Feature 4: _____

_____

_____

Feature 5: _____

_____

_____

Feature 6: _____

_____

_____

Feature 7: _____

_____

_____

Feature 8: _____

_____

_____

College Sales

Expedition Tool

College Characteristics

College name and location	Unique characteristics that create college identity (include phrases, symbols, and programs)

College Sales

Off You Go

Activity 2: College Brochure

> **Goal:** To create a brochure that markets your ideal college
>
> **Materials:** pencil, notebook paper, white or colored paper, clear tape, magazines, scissors, ruler, sticky notes

Directions

Part 1: Make the Layout

1. Make a tri-fold brochure layout by folding a sheet of notebook paper in thirds.

2. Open the sheet and number each of the six panels. Number 1 to 3 on the front and 4 to 6 on the back of the page (in pencil).

3. Next, fold the panel first from the right to the center and then from the left to the center. Panel 6 should be on top.

4. At the top of panel 6, write *Cover*.

5. At the top of panels 1 through 4, write *Text*.

6. At the top of panel 5, write *Back*.

Part 2: Creating the Text

1. Create a name for your ideal college. Write it below.

_____

2. Next, create a brief slogan (three to eight words) that identifies the most important characteristic of your school.

_____

_____

3. Look back at your list of six to eight features that you consider most important for the college you want to attend. Write one to two brief paragraphs describing each feature. Include descriptive details. Review the qualities of descriptive writing that you discovered looking at the other college brochures. Type your paragraphs using 12-point type. The text should be about 1.5 inches wide.

4. Type the name of the college and its slogan in 16- to 20-point type in lines that are 1.5 inches wide. This will allow the text to fit in your tri-fold layout.

(continued)

College Sales

Off You Go

5. The back panel in a brochure is used as a summary of the inside points. So, make a bulleted list of the six to eight most important features of your ideal college for the back panel of the brochure. Use 12-point type and keep the text 1.5 inches wide.

6. Print out all of your text.

Part 3: Putting It Together

1. Cut apart the paragraphs and headlines.

2. Using clear tape, place the text in panels 1 through 4. Leave space for potential illustrations or images.

3. Place the bulleted list of features on the back panel.

4. Cut out your ideal school's name and slogan, and tape it on the cover.

5. Look through the available magazines for any images to tape into the brochure.

6. Work with a partner and peer-review each other's brochures. Make suggestions for changes to clarify or expand the text. In addition, proofread your partner's materials and suggest changes in grammar, spelling, or punctuation.

7. Revise any text as needed and reprint.

8. Make a new tri-fold layout on a sheet of white or colored paper.

9. Create your final brochure with the revised text and images from your draft.

10. Form a small group and put a sticky note on your brochure. Pass your brochure around for others to view.

11. Review your classmates' brochures. On each sticky note, write a short comment about the brochure, noting what you liked about it.

12. After reading all the comments your classmates gave you, share with them very briefly what you learned from doing this project.

College Sales

Check Yourself!

Skill Check

1. What is a layout?

   _____

   _____

   _____

   _____

2. What is product identity and marketing?

   _____

   _____

   _____

   _____

   _____

3. What are selection criteria?

   _____

   _____

   _____

   _____

   _____

4. In literary terms, what is descriptive writing?

   _____

   _____

   _____

   _____

5. Is conducting an interview a good way to obtain information? Why or why not?

   _____

   _____

   _____

   _____

College Sales

Check Yourself!

Self-Assessment and Reflection

Before You Go
- ❏ I understand the parts of a one-page layout that contribute to getting a message to the reader.
- ❏ I know what product identity means.

Off You Go
- ❏ I know how to analyze marketing material to identify the key features of a product.
- ❏ I know the style in which to write marketing information.
- ❏ I know how to create a marketing tri-fold brochure.

Do You Know?
- ❏ I can define the Lingo to Learn vocabulary terms for this project and give an example of each.
- ❏ I completed the Skill Check questions and carefully reviewed questions I did not answer correctly.

Reflection

1. What were the most challenging aspects of this project for you and why?

   _____

   _____

   _____

2. Which skills did this project help you develop?

   _____

   _____

   _____

3. If you did this project again, what might you do differently and why?

   _____

   _____

   _____

Taking a Stand

Overview
Students will recognize the problems of bullying at school, then create an information and action campaign to share with others.

Time
Total time: 9 to 10 hours
- **Before You Go—What Is Bullying?** two classes and 40 minutes of homework, pp. 112–116
- **Activity 1—Planning for Change:** one class and 40 minutes of homework, pp. 117–118
- **Activity 2—Communicating Ideas:** one class and 30 minutes of homework, pp. 119–120
- **Activity 3—Writing a Persuasive Essay:** three classes and 20 minutes of homework, pp. 121–124
- **Check Yourself! Skill Check** and **Self-Assessment and Reflection** worksheets: 30 minutes of class time or homework, pp. 125–126

Materials
- notebook
- computer with Internet access and PowerPoint software
- chart paper
- markers
- white paper
- copy of PowerPoint slide template

Skill Focus
- research
- essay and persuasive writing
- presentation skills

Prior Knowledge
- Internet searches
- sentence and paragraph composition

Team Formation
- Students work in pairs, as individuals, and as a whole class.

Taking a Stand

Lingo to Learn—Terms to Know
- **citation:** notation in a piece of writing about the source of a quote or an idea
- **Internet site reliability:** accuracy of the information presented in a Web site
- **persuasive writing:** writing that expresses an opinion and tries to convince or influence the reader
- **transition words:** words that help guide and connect ideas in a piece of writing

Suggested Steps

Preparation
- Review all the materials and activities for the expedition. Note printables that you'll need to copy.
- Research current literature to identify the types of problems that are related to bullying in schools.
- It might help to talk to other teachers and administrators about the problem to determine the level of concern.

Day 1
1. Have students complete a quickwrite, a short 5-minute written response to the following question: What is bullying, and what can be done about it?

2. Invite students to share their ideas, first with a partner and then with the whole class.

3. Come to an agreed-upon definition of what bullying is.

4. Discuss with students if they think bullying is a problem in their school.

5. Distribute **Before You Go: What Is Bullying?** (pp. 112–114), along with **Expedition Tool: Problems and Solutions** (p. 115) and **Expedition Tool: Web Site Reliability** (p. 116).

6. Have students write their ideas in the left column of the T-chart.

7. Students can share their ideas in pairs. Discuss ideas with the whole class and make a master list. Have students add any items they do not have to their list.

8. Student pairs can brainstorm how bullying can be stopped and fill out the right column of the T-chart.

9. Have students research bullying and take notes on what they find. They can use the Helpful Web Resources or find additional sites. Students should review the Expedition Tool on Web site reliability and recording citations.

Taking a Stand

Homework

If students have Internet access at home, they can continue to research bullying. Students can also research how other schools have successfully stopped bullying. Students should be sure to determine the reliability of all Web sites used and note a citation for each idea recorded.

Day 2

1. Have students work in groups of three.

2. Provide each group with a sheet of chart paper and some markers.

3. Explain that groups are to create a list of the top three strategies for preventing bullying at their school. Any citations of Web sites should be included on the charts.

4. Have groups share their ideas with the class. Each group can present their ideas and post them for the rest of the class to see. Together, make a class list of ideas and have students vote for the top three to five ideas.

5. Identify the ideas with the largest number of votes.

6. Distribute **Activity 1: Planning for Change** (p. 117) and **Expedition Tool: Steps to Stop Bullying** (p. 118).

7. Ask students to select one of the winning ideas on which to base an action plan. It will be helpful if all the ideas are selected by roughly the same number of students.

Homework

Have students complete the Expedition Tool and draft a five-step action plan for implementing their chosen idea in the school.

Day 3

1. Place all students who selected the same idea into a small group.

2. Assign tasks to each group member. One student is to write the group's ideas on a piece of chart paper. Another student acts as group facilitator, calling on individuals to add to the conversation. One of their members will present the group's ideas to the whole class.

3. Explain that the groups will chart a series of steps to be taken to implement the no-bullying plan.

4. Review all of the plans with the whole class.

5. Students can ask questions or suggest changes to others' plans.

Taking a Stand

6. Provide time for the small groups to review the suggestions and revise their plans. Each group decides how to divide the steps up between all the members of the group. Each group member will create a PowerPoint slide on his or her step of the plan.

7. Distribute **Activity 2: Communicating Ideas** (p. 119) and **Expedition Tool: PowerPoint Tips** (p. 120).

8. Select a template from PowerPoint for all students to use as the background and colors for their slides. Print one blank slide in color for sharing with them, or show it with a computer and projector. Make black and white copies of the slide for each student.

Homework

Students should use the Expedition Tool to help them create one or two slides on white paper for their portion of the action plan.

Day 4

1. Provide time for students to work in their small groups. Each student is to share his or her slides and gather feedback—positive and constructive suggestions from the group.

2. Distribute **Activity 3: Writing a Persuasive Essay** (p. 121) and **Expedition Tool: Persuading Others** (pp. 122–124).

3. Students can work in pairs to complete the T-chart showing arguments for and against taking the actions they have decided upon to prevent bullying.

4. Have students share their ideas with the whole class.

5. Students should select the three most persuasive reasons for taking action and the strongest arguments against taking action.

6. Review the outline form for a persuasive essay.

7. Review the list of transition words that can be used to connect ideas in a persuasive essay.

8. Read the sample persuasive essay, and have students identify the key parts of the essay: the opening, the key points for action with supporting evidence, the key points against action with refutation, and the summary.

9. Ask students if they can find any transition words. Have them point out and explain why the words were used.

10. Have each student outline a persuasive essay to convince others to take action. The outlines should be turned in for comment.

Taking a Stand

Homework

Students should revise slides as needed.

Day 5

1. Return the outlines to students.

2. Set up a process to allow students to meet one-on-one with you as support for their writing.

3. While students are writing, set up a schedule to allow students to rotate through using computers to input their revised slides into a single PowerPoint file.

4. If some students finish early, they can create slides to present the strongest arguments for taking action as the introduction for the PowerPoint.

5. Collect the essays. You might wish to select the top two and have them presented to the Parent Teacher Association.

Day 6

1. Allow time for students to practice the presentation with the PowerPoint slides. Each small group should have a mock run-through using their slides on paper.

2. Students can do the actual presentation for other students, parents, or the Parent Teacher Association. Group members should stand together while presenting their action plan. Each student should read his or her slide. Students should use a transition statement to justify why their step is the next one.

Final Day

1. Have students complete the **Check Yourself! Skill Check** questions (p. 125).

2. Check and review answers.

3. Have students complete the **Check Yourself! Self-Assessment and Reflection** worksheet (p. 126) and submit it (optional).

Project Management Tips and Notes

- It is easiest if there is access to more than one computer for creating the slides. However, rotating students to a single computer station will also work.
- Bullying can be a sensitive subject, as it can surface negative feelings toward some students who might be seen as bullies. It may be helpful to have the school psychologist or counselor attend the opening classes when the topic is being discussed.

Taking a Stand

- Often parents do not recognize that bullying goes on in almost all schools. It might be helpful to send a note home to parents giving them information on Web sites to visit as students begin working on the project.

Suggested Assessment

Use the Project Assessment Rubric or the following point system:

Team and class participation	10 points
Before You Go	10 points
Activity 1	25 points
Activity 2	10 points
Activity 3	25 points
PowerPoint presentation	15 points
Self-Assessment and Reflection	5 points

Extension Activities

- Students can create a one-page handout to accompany the talk.
- Students can write a news release for the newspaper about the presentation.
- Students can create a background section to the report that provides more statistics about bullying.
- Students can create a new design for the slides and add images, animation, or Web site references.
- Students can create a video on bullying and the action students want to take.
- Students can create a television show to be broadcast on the local access channel.

Taking a Stand

Common Core State Standards Connection

Reading—Informational Text: Integration of Knowledge and Ideas

RI.6.7. Integrate information presented in different media or formats (e.g., visually, quantitatively) as well as in words to develop a coherent understanding of a topic or issue.

Writing: Text Types and Purposes

W.6.1, W.7.1, W.8.1. Write arguments to support claims with clear reasons and relevant evidence.

Writing: Research to Build and Present Knowledge

W.6.7, W.7.7. Conduct short research projects to answer a question, drawing on several sources....

W.8.7. Conduct short research projects to answer a question (including a self-generated question), drawing on several sources....

W.6.8. Gather relevant information from multiple print and digital sources; assess the credibility of each source; and quote or paraphrase the data and conclusions of others while avoiding plagiarism and providing basic bibliographic information for sources.

W.7.8, W.8.8. Gather relevant information from multiple print and digital sources, using search terms effectively; assess the credibility and accuracy of each source; and quote or paraphrase the data and conclusions of others while avoiding plagiarism and following a standard format for citation.

W.6.9, W.7.9, W.8.9. Draw evidence from literary or informational texts to support analysis, reflection, and research.

Answer Key

Check Yourself! Skill Check

1. An action plan is the steps needed to get something done.

2. Persuasive writing is writing that expresses an opinion and tries to convince or influence the reader.

3. Transition words can be used in persuasive writing to connect ideas.

4. A persuasive essay should begin with an introduction that explains the issue. This should be followed by the key points in support of the position, including specific data that might affirm the point. This would be followed by information that refutes the main arguments against the idea. Finally, there is a conclusion that restates the issue, the position, and the best supporting point.

Taking a Stand

Expedition Overview

Challenge

It's time to take action! You will create an action plan to stop bullying in your school. Then you will make a PowerPoint presentation showing the steps of the action plan and write a persuasive essay to present to others.

Objectives

- To learn about persuasive writing
- To learn to communicate to an audience
- To learn how to create an action plan in support of accomplishing a task

Project Activities

Before You Go

- What Is Bullying?

Off You Go

- Activity 1: Planning for Change
- Activity 2: Communicating Ideas
- Activity 3: Writing a Persuasive Essay

Expedition Tools

- Problems and Solutions
- Web Site Reliability
- Steps to Stop Bullying
- PowerPoint Tips
- Persuading Others

Other Materials Needed

- pencil
- notebook
- computer with Internet access and PowerPoint software
- chart paper
- markers
- white paper
- copy of PowerPoint slide template

Taking a Stand

Expedition Overview

Lingo to Learn—Terms to Know
- citation
- Internet site reliability
- persuasive writing
- transition words

Helpful Web Resources
- Department of Health & Human Services—Stop Bullying
  http://stopbullying.gov/
- It's My Life (PBS Kids)—Bullies: What Is Bullying?
  http://pbskids.org/itsmylife/friends/bullies/
- Pacer Center's Kids Against Bullying
  www.pacerkidsagainstbullying.org
- Scholastic—Writing Workshop: Persuasive Writing
  http://teacher.scholastic.com/activities/writing/conduct.asp?topic=Persuasive
- TeensHealth—Dealing With Bullying
  www.kidshealth.org/teen/your_mind/problems/bullies.html

Taking a Stand

Before You Go

What Is Bullying?

Goal:	To understand what bullying is
Materials:	notebook, computer with Internet access
Tools:	Problems and Solutions, Web Site Reliability

Directions

1. What is the definition of *bullying*? Write your ideas below. Be prepared to discuss your ideas with the class.

_____

_____

_____

_____

_____

_____

_____

2. What are some problems caused by bullying? Write your ideas in the left column of the T-chart in **Expedition Tool: Problems and Solutions.** Be prepared to discuss your ideas with a partner and then with the class.

3. With a partner, brainstorm how the behaviors of bullying could be stopped. Put your ideas in the right column of the T-chart.

4. Research bullying online according to your teacher's instructions. Use the Helpful Web Resources or other reliable Web sites that you find on your own. Use **Expedition Tool: Web Site Reliability** to help you determine the reliability or accuracy of Internet sites.

5. Note the information you find in the space below. Be sure to cite your information sources. Include the title of the Web page and the name of the organization that sponsored the Web site.

Taking a Stand

Before You Go

Notes on Bullying

Notes: _____

_____

_____

_____

_____

_____

_____

Source citation: _____

Web page title: _____

URL: _____

Organization: _____

Notes: _____

_____

_____

_____

_____

_____

_____

Source citation: _____

Web page title: _____

URL: _____

Organization: _____

(continued)

Taking a Stand

Before You Go

Notes: _____

_____

_____

_____

_____

_____

_____

_____

Source citation: _____

Web page title: _____

URL: _____

Organization: _____

Notes: _____

_____

_____

_____

_____

_____

_____

_____

Source citation: _____

Web page title: _____

URL: _____

Organization: _____

Taking a Stand

Expedition Tool

Problems and Solutions

Problems caused by bullying	How to stop bullying

Taking a Stand

Expedition Tool

Web Site Reliability

What type of site is it?
- If the URL ends in *.gov,* it is a state or federal government department.
- If the URL ends in *.edu,* it is a school or university.
- If the URL ends in *.org,* it is an organization.
- If the URL ends in *.com,* it is a commercial business.

Who created the Web page?
- Find the "about this site" section of the Web page.
- Look at the bottom of the home page.
- Read the site to determine if the materials were created by an expert, an entity with a biased opinion, or a student new to the topic.

Is the site current?
- Look for a date at the bottom of the Web page.
- Check links to see if they function. (Broken links are a sign that the author of the Web page is no longer taking care of the site.)

Is the material copyrighted?
- Check to see if there is a copyright symbol on the page.
- Be sure to check the use policy regarding any written materials or images you wish to use.
- Most written materials on a government Web site are copyright-free. However, the government site might be linked to another site, or the site might have received permission to post an article that is copyrighted.
- Always record in your notes where you found the material and who the author is.
- If you use the ideas presented in the materials, it is best if you cite the original author. Normally you would place the author's last name in the body of your text.
- At the end of your report, you should create a bibliography in which you put information for each source—the author's name, the title of the publication, the publisher, the Web site address, and the date you accessed the information.

Sample citation in a report:
Bullying isn't just physical. It can also be verbal and social (Department of Health & Human Services).

Bibliography entry:
Department of Health & Human Services. "What Is Bullying?" StopBullying.gov http://stopbullying.gov/topics/what_is_bullying/index.html (accessed January 18, 2012).

Taking a Stand

Off You Go

Activity 1: Planning for Change

> **Goal:** To learn how to write an action plan to accomplish a goal
>
> **Materials:** chart paper, markers
>
> **Tool:** Steps to Stop Bullying

Directions

1. You will work in teams of three.

2. On chart paper, make a list of the top three strategies for preventing bullying at your school. Include any Web site references on your charts.

3. Share your ideas with the class. Together, make a class list of ideas and vote for the top three ideas.

4. Select one of the top three ideas. Create an action plan with five steps to reach your goal to stop bullying.

5. Start by entering how you plan to stop bullying at your school at the top of **Expedition Tool: Steps to Stop Bullying.** Since you hope to have this accomplished by the end of your plan, you will work backwards from step 5, the successful end, to step 1, the first step.

Example

We will stop bullying by: informing all parents that some students are calling other students names during school, and this should stop.

Step 5 (the successful end): All parents have spoken to their children and told them that it is not right to call other people by bad names.

Taking a Stand

Expedition Tool

Steps to Stop Bullying

We will stop bullying by: _____

_____

Step 1: _____

_____

_____

Step 2: _____

_____

_____

Step 3: _____

_____

_____

Step 4: _____

_____

_____

Step 5: _____

_____

_____

Taking a Stand

Off You Go

Activity 2: Communicating Ideas

Goal:	To learn to create PowerPoint slides to communicate with an audience
Materials:	chart paper, markers, computer, PowerPoint software
Tool:	PowerPoint Tips

Directions

1. Get into a small group with the other students who selected the same action to stop bullying.

2. Each group member should have his or her own role. For instance, one student can write the group's ideas on a piece of chart paper. Another student can act as group facilitator, calling on individuals to add to the conversation. Another student can present the group's ideas to the whole class.

3. Take turns suggesting steps from each person's action plan. Other students can suggest a different first step, or revise the original suggestion. Continue until all the steps have been discussed and recorded. The group should have no more than five steps.

4. Present your group's ideas to the class for feedback. Review comments and suggestions, and make any necessary revisions to your action plan.

5. Each member or pair of members of the group is responsible for creating one PowerPoint slide on one step of the action plan. Use the guidelines in **Expedition Tool: PowerPoint Tips** to help you as you design the slide.

6. Once you are given a template upon which to create your slide, type the text you want to use in the appropriate size and width, and paste it into the template.

7. Add any copyright-free images you find.

Taking a Stand

Expedition Tool

PowerPoint Tips

1. Make statements short and bulleted.

2. Use at least 18-point font for text.

3. Use up to 36-point font for headlines.

4. Text should be no wider than 7.5 inches.

5. Use contrasting colors between background and text to be sure text is easily readable.

6. Do not add too much activity to text.

7. Add one high-quality image if available.

8. Be sure any text or image that you want the audience to read is large enough to be seen from the back of the room.

9. Remember your audience. Design your slide and write your text so your audience will easily understand your point. Do not use terms your audience will not be familiar with.

Taking a Stand

Off You Go

Activity 3: Writing a Persuasive Essay

Goal:	To learn to write a persuasive essay
Materials:	notebook, computer, PowerPoint software
Tool:	Persuading Others

Directions

1. With a partner, complete the first column of the table in the **Persuading Others Expedition Tool.** Write the reasons why you and the class decided the actions you are proposing are the best ones to take to prevent bullying in your school.

2. In the second column, write the reasons you think people might not want to take these actions.

3. Share your ideas with the class. Choose the three most persuasive reasons for taking action, and the two strongest arguments against taking action.

4. Review the parts of a persuasive essay in the Expedition Tool.

5. Review the purpose of transition words. Look at the list of transition words that can be used to connect ideas in a persuasive essay.

6. Read the sample persuasive essay. Identify the following key parts of the essay:
   - opening
   - key points for action
   - supporting evidence
   - key points against action
   - summary

7. Identify any transition words and where they are used.

8. On a separate sheet of paper, outline a persuasive essay using transition words that will convince a reader to follow your action plan. Submit your outline for feedback.

9. Once your teacher has returned your outline, you can write your essay.

10. Write a statement to transition between the previous slide and your slide in the PowerPoint presentation of your class action plan.

11. Share your essay, and practice and give your PowerPoint presentation according to your teacher's instructions.

Taking a Stand

Expedition Tool

Persuading Others
Part 1: Building Your Argument

Reasons for taking the action	Reasons against taking the action

(continued)

Taking a Stand

Expedition Tool

Part 2: Outline of a Persuasive Essay

1. Introduction
   - briefly describe the issue
   - briefly state the opinion or action you are supporting

2. First key point
   - supporting evidence

3. Second key point
   - supporting evidence

4. Third key point
   - supporting evidence

5. Arguments against the idea
   - reasons they are incorrect

6. Conclusion
   - restate the issue
   - state why the action proposed is best
   - state the action you hope the audience will take because of being persuaded

Part 3: Transition Words

Transition words can be used in writing to connect ideas.

Transition words that compare/contrast:	Transition words that emphasize a point:
• similarly • likewise • on the other hand • although • otherwise • alternatively	• especially • for this reason • in fact
Transition words that clarify:	Transition words that summarize:
• for instance • in other words • additionally • let me explain • since	• finally • to conclude • therefore • because • results in

(continued)

Taking a Stand

Expedition Tool

Part 4: Sample Persuasive Writing

Dear Company Manager:

In past phone conversations, I explained to you why I wish to return your lawn sweeper. The ad I read claimed that the tool could pick up leaves from the lawn "without the backache of raking leaves." This was not the case. Your lawn sweeper was poorly designed. It would not work on our sloped lawn and was made of weak materials.

The design of this lawn sweeper did not even reduce the amount of backache. Since I have an injured back, I am quite aware of any stress placed upon it. The sweeper had a relatively small catch basket. Whenever it got full, I had to bend over and unhook a poorly designed hook system. Then I had to lift the entire basket filled with leaves and carry the awkward basket over to where I disposed of the leaves. Even with a good back, this bending and lifting would have resulted in backaches.

Alternatively, each time the basket was full, I could have pushed it across the lawn and tipped it to empty it. However, its wheels were so small that when it got full the basket bottom dragged on the ground. This made forward motion very difficult, again placing strain on my back. Additionally, when the sweeper was on any kind of slope, it was nearly impossible to move.

Finally, after all of this struggling, I was through only half of my lawn. I reached down to unhook the basket and the rubber cap on the metal spoke broke off. The spoke came out and will no longer stay in when I push the sweeper. The metal used to construct this sweeper was much too thin.

When I called, you said you were so surprised that I was unhappy with the sweeper. You said that everyone else spoke highly of the equipment. I notice you did not reference these comments in your ads. I must trust that you have actually spoken to these people. Since I trusted that your ad was truthful, however, I have a hard time trusting you on this point. You also asserted that perhaps I received a malfunctioning sweeper. However, I would have to argue that it was not a small defect that caused all these problems, but major design flaws.

To conclude, as I stated in our conversation, I believe your ad and Web site contain false advertising. I have outlined the weaknesses and poor quality of this equipment. It had metal that was too weak to withstand the task. The basket was poorly designed, and its attachment to the sweeper was cumbersome. As well, the wheel height was too low and did not allow for use on any slopes. I would like your company to pay to have this item shipped back to you and refund me the cost of the sweeper plus shipping and handling.

Regretfully and with a sore back,

Susan Jones

Taking a Stand

Check Yourself!

Skill Check

1. What is an action plan?

   _____

   _____

   _____

2. In literary terms, what is persuasive writing?

   _____

   _____

   _____

   _____

3. How are transition words used in persuasive writing?

   _____

   _____

   _____

   _____

4. Describe the main sections of a persuasive essay.

   _____

   _____

   _____

   _____

   _____

Taking a Stand

Check Yourself!

Self-Assessment and Reflection

Before You Go

- ❑ I understand what bullying is.
- ❑ I understand how to evaluate Web sites for reliability.
- ❑ I understand how to make citations and a bibliography.

Off You Go

- ❑ I can create an action plan to identify the steps to take in order to reach a goal.
- ❑ I know the parts of a persuasive essay.
- ❑ I know what transition words are and how to use them in persuasive writing.
- ❑ I know how to consider my audience when creating a PowerPoint slide.

Do You Know?

- ❑ I can define the Lingo to Learn vocabulary terms for this project and give an example of each.
- ❑ I completed the Skill Check questions and carefully reviewed questions I did not answer correctly.

Reflection

1. What were the most challenging aspects of this project for you and why?

   _____

   _____

   _____

2. Which skills did this project help you develop?

   _____

   _____

   _____

3. If you did this project again, what might you do differently and why?

   _____

   _____

   _____

Your Quest

Overview

Students will survey a store, either in person or online, and select a product type to research. They research similar items from different manufacturers, comparing price and quality. They seek product reviews and specifications. Students will then choose the best product and write a virtual product review. The review will explain why the product chosen is the best value for the money. Finally, students will build a WebQuest that allows someone else to do similar product research.

Time

Total time: 7 to 9 hours

- **Before You Go—Making Business Decisions:** one class period and 60 minutes of homework, pp. 137–139
- **Activity 1—Researching Your Product:** one class period and 45 minutes of homework, pp. 140–144
- **Activity 2—Summarizing Your Choice:** one class period and 20 minutes of homework, pp. 145–150
- **Activity 3—Building a WebQuest:** two class periods and 20 minutes of homework, pp. 151–154
- **Activity 4—Sharing What You Know (optional):** one class period and 20 minutes of homework, pp. 155–156
- **Check Yourself! Skill Check** and **Self-Assessment and Reflection** worksheets: 30 minutes of class time or homework, pp. 157–158

Materials

- notebook
- computer with Internet access
- copyright-free images

Skill Focus

- conducting research
- comparing and contrasting
- critical thinking
- business communication
- summarizing

Your Quest

Prior Knowledge
- familiarity with WebQuest construction helpful
- Internet searches

Team Formation
- Students work in pairs, as individuals, and as a whole class.

Lingo to Learn—Terms to Know
- **manufacturer:** a business that makes an item
- **product research:** tests done to products to assure they meet quality standards
- **product review:** an analysis of how well a product functions and meets its advertising claims
- **profit margin:** the amount of profit a business can make after it has paid all expenses connected to the sale of an item or a service
- **retailer:** a business that sells manufactured goods

Suggested Steps
Preparation
- Review all the materials and activities for the expedition. Note printables that you'll need to copy.
- If possible, contact a small-business owner who can come to class to discuss how purchasing decisions are made.
- Contact the computer instructor to arrange scheduling access to the computers for creating the WebQuests and doing the online product research. He or she might also be helpful in supporting the building of the WebQuests.
- Contact the librarian to see if he or she has any preferable techniques for assessing Web site quality. The librarian could also assist students in finding reputable product reviews from publications such as *Consumer Reports* and so forth.
- If you intend to have students visit local stores, it would be beneficial to inform parents about the project. There are also letters to the stores included. These are to help make staff more comfortable with the students' activities and then communicate students' findings at the end of the project. It might also be helpful to send a notice to the local chamber of commerce so that they are aware of the project.
- If you are using a free online WebQuest development site, you will need to register and create a password. This will then be usable by each student to create his or her own WebQuest. WebQuests will be under your registration, however, so you may want to identify the class along with your name to acknowledge their authorship.

Your Quest

Day 1

1. Explain the project to the students. They will select a business whose products they are interested in. Products could include clothing, hardware, automotive items, and so forth. Their task will be to create a WebQuest that will help others find the best products for the best price. Each student will write a virtual product review.

2. If possible, have a small-business owner come to class to describe the process of deciding what to buy for the store.

3. Distribute **Before You Go: Making Business Decisions** (p. 137) along with **Expedition Tool: Letter to Business Owner** (p. 138) and **Expedition Tool: Product Research Table** (p. 139).

4. Review the process students will go through when they visit a store of their choosing. Alternatively, students can go online to do their research via the store's Web site.

5. Create a table on a piece of chart paper that has columns for student name, store, and product. Keep this posted so students can see the products other students are researching.

6. Have students select a store in which they are interested. Students then select a product available in that store on which they will do comparative shopping research. Products can range from clothing items such as skirts, pairs of pants, sweaters, or coats, to equipment such as carburetors or electric drills. Be sure that the category is not too large. It is best to have three to five manufacturers for the product. Therefore, if it is a type of clothing, students should select a particular size and type, such as a women's winter dress coat in size 10. Alternatively, if it is a tool, students should select a specific size such as a ¾-inch electric drill (both battery and plug-in).

7. Each student enters his or her name and store on the chart paper.

8. Explain that it does not matter if more than one student goes to the same store. Students can also choose the same product. However, they should do their research independently.

9. Talk about how students are to visit the store or the store's Web site. Students can use **Expedition Tool: Product Research Table** (p. 139) to take notes on the types of products the store carries and its most common brands.

Homework

If students are visiting a store in person, they do so for homework and survey the store's product line. They complete the table in the Expedition Tool and select one product for their virtual product review.

Your Quest

Day 2

1. As students come to class, have them enter the product they decided to research in the table.

2. In groups of three, students are to share their store profiles and product comparisons. They can be grouped randomly, by store, or by self-selection.

3. Distribute **Activity 1: Researching Your Product** (p. 140) and **Expedition Tool: Product Data Research** (pp. 141–144).

4. Have students use the Internet to research three to five manufacturers of their selected product, compare specifications, and examine prices. They should keep track of the Web sites they visit that would be beneficial for another person to use while researching other products. They should also write a short annotation for each Web site.

Homework

Students should complete the Expedition Tool to summarize what they have found.

Day 3

1. Have students return to their small groups to share what they learned in their research, including any Web sites they think might be helpful to others in the group.

2. Create a table on chart paper, the blackboard, or an overhead. In one column, indicate the name of the product. In the next column, place the number of manufacturers the students found for each product. In the third column, indicate the price range for the items.

3. Direct students to work in small groups to examine the data and write three conclusions about it. For instance, students might conclude that there are more companies making clothes than making hardware or automotive items. Another idea might involve the relationship between the number of manufacturers and the range in prices.

4. Distribute **Activity 2: Summarizing Your Choice** (pp. 145–146), along with **Expedition Tool: Product Review Example** (pp. 147–148) and **Expedition Tool: Virtual Product Review** (pp. 149–150).

5. Have students read the sample reviews. Discuss with students the different parts of a product review.

6. Students should outline their own virtual product reviews.

7. In pairs, students share their outlines and receive comments on their decisions and their justification.

8. Have students revise their outlines as needed and begin writing their virtual product reviews.

Your Quest

Homework

Students should complete their virtual product reviews.

Day 4

1. Allow time for students to share their virtual product review with a partner and revise as necessary.

2. Have students find a second partner to proofread the review. Students should make any corrections necessary. Meet with each student one-on-one to provide support as needed.

3. Discuss WebQuests with students. A WebQuest is a guided use of the Internet, usually done in order to complete a task. Students will create a WebQuest that will allow another person to investigate products made by different manufacturers, find online reviews of those products, and make pricing comparisons.

4. Distribute **Activity 3: Building a WebQuest** (p. 151) and **Expedition Tool: What Is a WebQuest?** (pp. 152–154).

5. Access the Internet and have students go to one of the free WebQuest development sites such as Zunal (www.zunal.com), or use any school software to create a WebQuest.

6. With a computer projector, go through one of the WebQuests (there are many on the Zunal site), outlining the components while reviewing **Expedition Tool: What Is a WebQuest?** (pp. 152–154).

7. Students are to use a separate sheet of paper to write their WebQuest introduction, task, process, and conclusion.

8. Provide time for students to share their writing with a partner and revise it as necessary.

9. Have students share some of their writing with the whole class.

10. Students should make the list of Web sites for their WebQuest and find appropriate copyright-free images to use.

11. When all their materials are collected, students can log in and begin to build a WebQuest.

12. Students will create a digital form of **Expedition Tool: Virtual Product Review** (pp. 149–150). This will be uploaded as the worksheet portion of their WebQuest.

13. Before the end of class, have a few students share what they have created.

Homework

Students should continue to work on their WebQuest designs.

Your Quest

Day 5

1. Have students complete their WebQuests.

2. If students visited stores in person, distribute **Activity 4: Sharing What You Know** (p. 155) and **Expedition Tool: Letter of Thanks** (p. 156), which are optional activities. Students can complete the Expedition Tool, or they can write their own letters to the businesses where they did their surveys.

3. You can have students return to the store where they did their survey to deliver the thank-you letter, virtual product review, and WebQuest Web site address.

Final Day

1. Have students complete the **Check Yourself! Skill Check** questions (p. 157).

2. Check and review answers.

3. Have students complete the **Check Yourself! Self-Assessment and Reflection** worksheet (p. 158) and submit it (optional).

Project Management Tips and Notes

- It is easiest if there is access to more than one computer for creating the WebQuests. However, rotating students to a single computer station will also work.
- For English Language Learners, suggest that they first build their WebQuest in their native language before translating it into English to share with others.

Suggested Assessment

Use the Project Assessment Rubric or the following point system:

Team and class participation	10 points
Before You Go	15 points
Activity 1	15 points
Activity 2	35 points
Activity 3	20 points
Self-Assessment and Reflection	5 points

Your Quest

Extension Activities

- Students can survey their class to determine what types of product reviews would be most helpful and complete them.
- Students could learn to create their own Web page that has links to all the virtual product reviews.

Common Core State Standards Connection

Writing: Text Types and Purposes

W.6.2, W.7.2, W.8.2. Write informative/explanatory texts to examine a topic and convey ideas, concepts, and information through the selection, organization, and analysis of relevant content.

    b. Develop the topic with relevant, well-chosen facts, definitions, concrete details, quotations, or other information and examples.*

    d. Use precise language and domain-specific vocabulary to inform about or explain the topic.

Writing: Production and Distribution of Writing

W.6.4, W.7.4, W.8.4. Produce clear and coherent writing in which the development, organization, and style are appropriate to task, purpose, and audience.

Writing: Research to Build and Present Knowledge

W.6.7, W.7.7. Conduct short research projects to answer a question, drawing on several sources....

W.8.7. Conduct short research projects to answer a question (including a self-generated question), drawing on several sources....

Writing: Range of Writing

W.6.10, W.7.10, W.8.10. Write routinely over extended time frames (time for research, reflection, and revision) and shorter time frames (a single sitting or a day or two) for a range of discipline-specific tasks, purposes, and audiences.

Teacher Page

Answer Key
Check Yourself! Skill Check

1. Doing research is looking for the facts about a topic. This includes finding facts from different sources, noting where you got them, and often comparing them.

2. Comparing and contrasting is finding the similarities and differences between two items.

3. Critical thinking is analyzing presented facts in order to come to a decision about what to do.

4. Business communications can take different forms. It can be the way an item is advertised. It can also be correspondence between people regarding business topics. It is usually formal and does not contain any slang words.

5. Summarizing is drawing conclusions about what you have been studying, then writing or speaking about them briefly, including only the most important details.

Your Quest

Expedition Overview

Challenge

Your quest awaits you! Your mission is to survey a store of your choice and identify what products its sells. You will select one type of product and research how it varies among different manufacturers. Then you will write a virtual product review describing the best product for the money and create a WebQuest that anyone could use to do product research.

Objectives

- To learn about sales of products in stores
- To learn how to research and write a virtual product review
- To learn how to create a WebQuest

Project Activities

Before You Go

- Making Business Decisions

Off You Go

- Activity 1: Researching Your Product
- Activity 2: Summarizing Your Choice
- Activity 3: Building a WebQuest
- Activity 4 (optional): Sharing What You Know

Expedition Tools

- Letter to Business Owner
- Product Research Table
- Product Data Research
- Product Review Example
- Virtual Product Review
- What Is a WebQuest?
- Letter of Thanks

Other Materials Needed

- notebook
- pencil or pen
- computer with Internet access
- copyright-free images

Your Quest

Expedition Overview

Lingo to Learn—Terms to Know
- manufacturer
- product research
- product review
- profit margin
- retailer

Helpful Web Resources
- CNET
  www.cnet.com
- Consumer Search
  www.consumersearch.com
- ConsumerReports.org
  www.consumerreports.org/cro/index.htm
- Phoenix OS/2 Society—How to Write a Product Review
  www.possi.org/extended_attributes/2000/11/bitstream/view

Your Quest

Before You Go

Making Business Decisions

Goal:	To do a survey of a store to find out what is sold there and select a product to research
Materials:	notebook, pencil, computer with Internet access (optional)
Tools:	Letter to Business Owner, Product Research Table

Directions

1. Select a store that is easy for you to visit, either in person or online, and has products that you are interested in.

2. On the chart made by your teacher, write your name and the store you have selected.

3. If you are visiting a store in person, complete **Expedition Tool: Letter to Business Owner** by adding the date and your school's contact information. This is what you will provide the business in order to explain the project.

4. Visit the store you chose, or explore the store's Web site according to your teacher's instructions. If you visit a store in person, remember to bring your letter explaining the project with you.

5. Survey the store and take notes using **Expedition Tool: Product Research Table.**

6. Record the store's name and the different departments it has. If it is a hardware store, for instance, you might write *paint, garden supplies, building tools, electric supply,* and so forth. If it is a clothing store, you might write *women's dresses, women's skirts, women's shirts, men's suits, men's coats, men's shirts,* and so forth.

7. Select one product to research and write it down. Be specific enough about your product so that you are only comparing three to five manufacturers (makers) of the product. For instance, if choosing a type of clothing, select one size and one material (such as short wool skirts in size 12). If you are selecting a type of hardware, choose one specific product, such as a ¾-inch electric drill.

8. In the Expedition Tool, record the product, the names of the different manufacturers that make the product, and the various prices.

9. In class, share your store profiles and product information with your group.

Your Quest

Expedition Tool

Letter to Business Owner

Date: _____

Dear Business Owner:

In my English language arts class, we are doing a project to learn about writing product reviews. I would like to do a survey of your store and write a virtual product review on one of the items you sell.

To complete my project, I will research this item and look at differences among items made by different manufacturers. I will identify which I think is the best value. I will be recording the steps I take to do my research and creating a WebQuest online about my process.

After I have completed the process, I can share the virtual product review with you and give you the Web address for my WebQuest in case you want to use it for future research.

Please use the following contact information if you have any questions about the project:

Teacher name: _____

School name: _____

School phone number: _____

Gratefully,

_____

Your Quest

Expedition Tool

Product Research Table

Store name: _____

Departments: _____

_____

_____

_____

Product: _____

Product	Manufacturer	Price
Total number:	Total number:	Range:

Your Quest

Off You Go

Activity 1: Researching Your Product

Goal:	To research similar items that are made by different manufacturers to determine which has the best features and value for customers
Materials:	computer with Internet access
Tool:	Product Data Research

Directions

1. Use the Internet to research the product you selected.

2. Determine what is different about similar products made by three to five different manufacturers.

3. Find expert product reviews on each item to determine how well the product meets its claims.

4. Find the manufacturer's list price for each item.

5. Keep a record of all of the Web sites you visit. You will use them for building your WebQuest. These will help someone else do the same type of research you are doing for another similar product. Write a short description of what information is available at the Web site when you record the name and Web address.

Your Quest

Expedition Tool

Product Data Research

Product: _____

1. Manufacturer: _____

   Manufacturer's Web site: _____

   Product specifications: _____

   _____

   _____

   _____

   _____

   _____

   Manufacturer's list price: _____

   Product review: _____

   _____

   _____

   _____

   _____

   _____

   Reviewer: _____

   Reviewer's Web site: _____

(*continued*)

Your Quest

Expedition Tool

2. Manufacturer: _____

   Manufacturer's Web site: _____

   Product specifications: _____

   _____

   _____

   _____

   _____

   _____

   Manufacturer's list price: _____

   Product review: _____

   _____

   _____

   _____

   _____

   _____

   Reviewer: _____

   Reviewer's Web site: _____

3. Manufacturer: _____

   Manufacturer's Web site: _____

   Product specifications: _____

   _____

   _____

   _____

   _____

   Manufacturer's list price: _____

(continued)

Expeditions in Your Classroom: English Language Arts, Grades 6–8   © Walch Education

Your Quest

Expedition Tool

Product review: _____

_____

_____

_____

_____

_____

Reviewer: _____

Reviewer's Web site: _____

4. Manufacturer: _____

Manufacturer's Web site: _____

Product specifications: _____

_____

_____

_____

_____

_____

Manufacturer's list price: _____

Product review: _____

_____

_____

_____

_____

_____

_____

Reviewer: _____

Reviewer's Web site: _____

(*continued*)

Your Quest

Expedition Tool

5. Manufacturer: _____

Manufacturer's Web site: _____

Product specifications: _____

_____

_____

_____

_____

Manufacturer's list price: _____

Product review: _____

_____

_____

_____

_____

Reviewer: _____

Reviewer's Web site: _____

Your Quest

Off You Go

Activity 2: Summarizing Your Choice

Goal:	To select the best product for the price and write a justification in a virtual product review
Materials:	pencil, notebook, computer with Internet access
Tools:	Product Review Example, Virtual Product Review

Directions

What Is a Product Review?

A product review is an essay that describes how well a product made by one manufacturer compares to one made by a different manufacturer. It is a way to summarize why you would choose one product over another. In most instances, the author has actually used each product. Since that will not be possible in this project, you will be writing a virtual product review.

1. Read **Expedition Tool: Product Review Example** to become familiar with virtual product reviews.

2. Think about the customers who probably shop at the store you investigated. Imagine that you are writing a letter to them advising them which product to buy.

3. At the top of **Expedition Tool: Virtual Product Review,** identify the product you have selected, its manufacturer, and the manufacturer's Web site. Then complete each section of the product review as follows:

   • **Introduction:** This is an overview that should generally describe the product and why you like it.

   • **Comparison of features:** This should indicate why the features of your selection are better than those of the competition.

   • **Comparison of value:** Explain why you think your selected product has the most features at the best cost. It might not be the cheapest or the most expensive option, but you are recommending it because it has the most features needed for the best price. You can also write which product you might choose if money was no object, or which you might choose if you had less to spend.

   • **Product features:** List the features the manufacturer feels are important qualities about the product. This is usually a bulleted list of features often found on the manufacturer's Web site, in its advertising, or on the tag or box of the product.

(continued)

Your Quest

Off You Go

- **Product specifications:** Here write a detailed description of the item you decided was the best choice. These are the technical details a customer might want to know. These can include such things as the type of fabric for an item of clothing or the weight of a tool.

- **Online comparison shopping:** This is a comparison of costs at various online retailers. Use the Internet to compare prices for the specific product you chose. Then complete the table. Under each store, note the store's Web site, the shipping costs, and the price. Be sure to put a date above the table indicating when the prices were effective. Remember to keep a record of all of the Web sites you visit.

Your Quest

Expedition Tool

Product Review Example

Part 1: Product Overview

The Sony Digital Camera DSC-W7 is a wonderful little camera for the money! You'll get beautiful picture quality and little lag time between shots. The compact size fits easily in your pocket or purse so you can carry the camera with you at all times. The rechargeable battery holds the charge for a long period of time. The camera has good auto scene modes for beginners, but even professionals will love the image quality. The menus are a little hard to get used to and not as easy to use as on some other brands, but once you learn where everything is it gets easier. It does take a memory stick, so you'll have to change card types if you're currently using any camera that isn't a Sony. Pros far outweigh the cons!

Part 2: Comparison of Features and Value

The best thing about the Sony is the image quality. In fact, I think the image quality of the Sony far exceeded that of most other handheld digital cameras. In some cases it beat the Canon 10D I used in the past in shadow detail. The Sony-made sensor is available in some truly wonderful cameras like the Canon G6, Olympus, Casio, and others. If you like the image quality but aren't sold on the Sony DSC-W7, you should take a look at some of the other cameras that use the same sensor. Image quality is a combination of the sensor, the lens, and the camera's processor, and Sony's overall package is truly spectacular.

It's hard to say anything about this camera that would keep you from buying it. The main issue for me would be a lack of artistic control, the result of not having aperture or shutter priority. That probably will not even affect you, because it relates to my style of photography. It doesn't make this camera inferior to any other competing camera. For most people, this could be the camera that provides the most reliable source of family memories. They may never need to buy another camera.

Part 3: Sample Features

Featuring

8.1 MP resolution
Carl Zeiss 3X optical zoom
Face detection
Double anti-blur solution
HD output to your HDTV (HDTV connector cable sold separately)
In-camera retouching
31 MB internal memory
2.5-inch LCD screen
Up to 350-shot power

(continued)

Your Quest

Expedition Tool

Part 4: Product Description

The DSC-W7 Cyber-shot® camera zooms ahead of the pack in the world of compact cameras. The enhanced 7.2 Megapixel CCD produces sharp images, even for large prints—images you can preview easily with the 2.5-inch LCD display. Special noise reduction and auto-focus features improve your shots, while the histogram display makes it easier to use. Seven unique Scene Selection modes provide automatic presets for portraits by moonlight or candlelight. Finally, with its Carl Zeiss zoom lens and energy-efficient operation, you'll get more from your shots—as well as more time for them. The Sony not only has an automatic setting to ensure your images turn out their best, but for the more adventurous photographer, you can also use the manual settings. With manual exposure and histogram display control, you get improved image quality and greater control. Its amazingly quick shutter speed gives you the power to capture more of your favorite shots in less time, while the automatic and manual aperture controls let you decide the best look and feel to your digital images.

The Sony camera is the perfect choice for photo enthusiasts looking to add a professional feel to their digital pictures. Using the Sony VAD-WA Lens Adapter, select from a number of lenses right for any situation. Add the 30mm, Wide-Angle or Telephoto Lens to the Cyber-shot® W7 and capture the picture you have been looking for.

Adapted from Amazon.com: http://www.amazon.com/Sony-Cybershot-DSC-W7-Digital-Optical/dp/B0007S8C7I

Your Quest

Expedition Tool

Virtual Product Review

Product: _____

Manufacturer: _____

Web site: _____

Introduction: _____

_____

_____

_____

Comparison of features: _____

_____

_____

_____

Comparison of value: _____

_____

_____

_____

Product features: _____

_____

_____

_____

Product specifications: _____

_____

_____

_____

_____

(continued)

Your Quest

Expedition Tool

Online Comparison Shopping

Prices effective: _____

Store				
Store's Web site				
Price of product				
Shipping costs				

Your Quest

Off You Go

Activity 3: Building a WebQuest

Goal:	To create a WebQuest based on what you learned doing your virtual product review
Materials:	computer with Internet access, copyright-free images
Tool:	What Is a WebQuest?

Directions

1. Read Expedition Tool: What Is a WebQuest?

2. Access the Internet and go to a free WebQuest development site such as Zunal (www.zunal.com).

3. Go through some existing WebQuests to see the format.

4. On a separate sheet of paper, write a draft of the sections of your WebQuest—your introduction, task, process with Web sites, and conclusion.

5. Note any ideas for images that you could put in your WebQuest.

6. Share your writings with a partner. Revise your work based on your partner's comments.

7. Go to a Web site that has free clip art, or do an image search within a .gov domain for images to download and put in your WebQuest (these are usually copyright-free). Your school might also have some copyright-free images to use.

8. Follow your teacher's directions for registering on the Web site (www.zunal.com/register-form.php), or log in and then begin to build a WebQuest portion of the Web site.

9. Enter the information and upload the images as requested.

Your Quest

Expedition Tool

What Is a WebQuest?

A WebQuest is a guided use of the Internet to answer a question. It is created by making a Web page that introduces the WebQuest. The WebQuest then provides a series of questions and Web sites that can be used to answer the questions.

There are six parts to a WebQuest:
- **Introduction:** a welcome and general overview of the task
- **Task:** the specific details of the WebQuest
- **Process:** the plan of action with corresponding Web sites
- **Conclusion:** a brief summary, usually congratulatory in tone, that wraps up the project
- **Evaluation:** a rubric that participants can use to determine how well they did on creating their virtual product review
- **Teacher page:** identifies the national standards addressed by the project

Introduction

This WebQuest is to prepare a virtual product review. The product review will be helpful in comparing similar items made by different manufacturers in order to decide which is the best to buy.

Task

You will be selecting one electronics item to review. You will compare the same types of products made by different companies. You want to discover which product has the best features for the money. You will then write a product review.

The steps to complete a product review include the following:

- Identify specific products, their manufacturers, and their list prices.
- Compare the features and value of the products.
- Select the product you think is best, and compare prices at various online retail stores.

Process
- Step 1: Download the virtual product review.
- Step 2: Explore the Web sites given.
- Step 3: Complete the virtual product review with the information from the Web sites.

Conclusion

Congratulations! You can make a recommendation on what to buy based on factual research.

Your Quest

Expedition Tool

Evaluation

The following is a sample rubric you can modify for your project:

Student will be graded individually on the following:	Beginning 1	Developing 2	Very Good 3	Exemplary 4	Score
Product comparison on features	Student did not compare the features of two or more products.	Student compared two products with some inaccuracies.	Student compared at least two products completely.	Student compared more than two products very effectively.	30%
Product comparison on value	Student did not compare the value of any products (the features for the cost).	Student compared the values of two products but did so inaccurately or incompletely.	Student compared the value of at least two products completely and accurately.	Student thoroughly compared more than two products.	30%
Mechanics	Student had more than 8 errors in spelling, punctuation, and capitalization.	Student had 5 to 8 errors in spelling, punctuation, and capitalization.	Student had no errors in spelling, punctuation, and capitalization.	Students had no grammatical errors, and sentences were very well structured.	20%
Presentation	Student's work was not legible or clear. Statements were unclear.	Student's work was somewhat legible but was not clear or neat. Statements were slightly confusing.	Student's work was well organized. Statements were short and factual.	Student had clear, descriptive statements that were well thought out.	20%

Your Quest

Expedition Tool

Teacher page

Copy the following information onto the teacher's page:

Common Core State Standards Connection
Writing: Text Types and Purposes

W.6.2, W.7.2, W.8.2. Write informative/explanatory texts to examine a topic and convey ideas, concepts, and information through the selection, organization, and analysis of relevant content.

    b.   Develop the topic with relevant, well-chosen facts, definitions, concrete details, quotations, or other information and examples.*

    d.   Use precise language and domain-specific vocabulary to inform about or explain the topic.

Writing: Production and Distribution of Writing

W.6.4, W.7.4, W.8.4. Produce clear and coherent writing in which the development, organization, and style are appropriate to task, purpose, and audience.

Writing: Research to Build and Present Knowledge

W.6.7, W.7.7. Conduct short research projects to answer a question, drawing on several sources....

W.8.7. Conduct short research projects to answer a question (including a self-generated question), drawing on several sources....

Writing: Range of Writing

W.6.10, W.7.10, W.8.10. Write routinely over extended time frames (time for research, reflection, and revision) and shorter time frames (a single sitting or a day or two) for a range of discipline-specific tasks, purposes, and audiences.

Your Quest

Off You Go

Activity 4: Sharing What You Know

Goal:	To write a letter to the store you surveyed to communicate the results of the project, including your virtual product review and the WebQuest address
Materials:	computer or pen
Tool:	Letter of Thanks

Directions

1. Now that you have completed your virtual product review and created your WebQuest, you can return to the store you surveyed and share what you have learned.

2. Complete **Expedition Tool: Letter of Thanks.** Address the letter as appropriate and add the date.

3. Specify the type of product and the name and manufacturer of the specific product that you selected as the best value.

4. Add the Web address of your WebQuest.

5. Add your teacher's name and the school's phone number so you can be contacted if needed.

6. Attach a copy of your virtual product review.

7. Sign your name at the bottom, and print your name under your signature.

Your Quest

Expedition Tool

Letter of Thanks

Date: _____

Dear _____ ,

Thank you so much for letting me conduct research on your store and the products you carry.
For my project, I compared the features and value of similar products made by different
manufacturers. I was unable to try the products, but I did read product reviews by
others who had tested the products.

I have written a virtual product review detailing my findings. Attached is my virtual
product review on _____ .

I found the _____ manufactured by

_____ to be the best product of its type.

In doing my research, I went through a specific research process. I reviewed many Web
sites and created a WebQuest using some of these Web sites in case others might want to do
research of their own. You can find my WebQuest at: _____ .

Please let me know if you have any questions. I can be reached through my teacher:

_____ at _____ .

Gratefully,

_____

Your Quest

Check Yourself!

Skill Check

1. What does it mean to do research?

   _____

   _____

   _____

2. When reviewing something, what does it mean to compare and contrast?

   _____

   _____

   _____

3. What is critical thinking?

   _____

   _____

   _____

   _____

4. What are business communications?

   _____

   _____

   _____

   _____

5. What is summarizing?

   _____

   _____

   _____

Your Quest

Check Yourself!

Self-Assessment and Reflection

Before You Go
- ❑ I understand how to survey a store's products, either in person or online.
- ❑ I know how to identify the types of people who shop in the store.
- ❑ I know how to select an item to research, and record the names and brands of the different types of this product that are sold in the store.

Off You Go
- ❑ I can compare the features of two or more items made by different manufacturers.
- ❑ I know how to compare the prices of the various items I am studying.
- ❑ I know how to determine the product that is the best value for the money.
- ❑ I know how to write up a virtual product review for the product I selected.
- ❑ I know how to create a WebQuest about the process I used to write a virtual product review.

Do You Know?
- ❑ I can define the Lingo to Learn vocabulary terms for this project and give an example of each.
- ❑ I completed the Skill Check questions and carefully reviewed questions I did not answer correctly.

Reflection

1. What were the most challenging aspects of this project for you and why?

   _____

   _____

   _____

2. Which skills did this project help you develop?

   _____

   _____

   _____

3. If you did this project again, what might you do differently and why?

   _____

   _____

   _____

Finding Your Roots

Overview

Students investigate the genealogy of their classmates, learn about traditions from different cultures, and describe a family tradition to a pen pal.

Time

Total time: 5 hours
- **Before You Go—Family Heritage:** one class and 60 minutes of homework, pp. 167–169
- **Activity 1—Holiday Traditions:** three classes and 40 minutes of homework, pp. 170–174
- **Check Yourself! Skill Check** and **Self-Assessment and Reflection** worksheets: 30 minutes of class time or homework, pp. 175–176

Materials

- notebook
- pencil

Skill Focus

- writing for a purpose
- editing and revising writing
- cross-cultural communication

Prior Knowledge

- basic grammar and mechanics
- peer editing

Team Formation

- Students work in pairs, as individuals, and as a whole class.

Lingo to Learn—Terms to Know

- **cultural heritage:** traditions, customs, beliefs, art, language, and other aspects of culture passed on from generation to generation
- **genealogy:** a study of a family with the identification of ancestors
- **immigration:** movement into a different area, region, or country one is not a native of in order to live

Finding Your Roots

Suggested Steps

Preparation

- Review all the materials and activities for the expedition. Note printables that you'll need to copy.
- Examine your family's heritage to share with students. Complete **Expedition Tool: Charting Family** (pp. 168–169) and make an overhead, or prepare to project it for the class to see.
- It might be helpful to ask a social studies teacher to give a brief presentation on immigration in the United States.
- If you plan to share the results of the project with the school board, contact them to inform them of the project and set a time to deliver the results. Alternatively, you could invite them to the first and last class to express their interest in the information.

Day 1

1. Describe the project to the class. Students will examine the origins and cultural heritage of their families. They will compile the information on where their families came from and recognize all the nationalities the class represents. They will also describe traditions for holidays that are celebrated by their families.

2. If you have members of the school board attend class, have them discuss why this information is helpful to them.

3. Discuss the terms *immigration, genealogy, cultural heritage,* and *traditions.* Have students complete a quickwrite, a short 5-minute written response to the following question: Why are family traditions important?

4. Invite students to share some ideas.

5. Distribute **Before You Go: Family Heritage** (p. 167) and **Expedition Tool: Charting Family** (pp. 168–169).

6. Share your completed Expedition Tool as a model.

7. Ask students to interview a relative in order to complete the information on their family heritage. Be sure to encourage them to include traditions that relate to holidays.

Homework

Students should complete the tables in the Expedition Tool.

Finding Your Roots

Day 2

1. Work with the whole class to compile results. Make a table of all the states and countries students' families came from. Indicate the number of students who have ancestors from each state and country. Finally, list the special holiday traditions the family has. Make a bar chart on the blackboard or an overhead to illustrate the heredity of the students. Put the countries and states on the bottom and the number of students along the side.

2. Distribute **Activity 1: Holiday Traditions** (pp. 170–171), along with **Expedition Tool: Guide to Writing Letters** (p. 172) and **Expedition Tool: Sample Letter** (pp. 173–174).

3. Have students work in pairs and describe family traditions to each other. Allow partners to ask questions so students can clarify or expand descriptions.

4. Review **Expedition Tool: Guide to Writing Letters** (p. 170) with students. Discuss how writing letters is similar to and different from other styles of writing the students have done. For instance, a letter must have good grammar, sentence structure, and organization, but it might also include more descriptions and feelings than some other forms of writing.

5. Ask students to submit two to three sentences describing the tradition they will write about in a letter to a pen pal. (The pen pal is a fictional person from another country.)

Homework

Have students complete the activity in preparation for their writing.

Day 3

1. Review **Expedition Tool: Sample Letter** (pp. 173–174) with students and go over the questions on the activity page.

2. Meet with students in writing conferences while they work on their letters.

3. When students complete their letters, direct them to find a partner who will read the letter and offer any suggestions for improvements.

4. Give students time to make final revisions to their letters.

Homework

Students should complete the final version of their letters if additional time is needed.

Finding Your Roots

Day 4

1. Have students read their letters to the whole class. Allow students to ask questions about the traditions described.

2. If desired, have members of the school board present to review the data collected and hear students' letters.

3. Collect the final letters and compile them into a booklet. The booklet can be shared with other students, parents, or members of the school board. Consider identifying actual pen pals and sending copies of the letters to them.

Final Day

1. Have students complete the **Check Yourself! Skill Check** questions (p. 175).

2. Check and review answers.

3. Have students complete the **Check Yourself! Self-Assessment and Reflection** worksheet (p. 176) and submit it (optional).

Project Management Tips and Notes

- Family heritage and immigration can be a sensitive issue for some students. Some students may not know that their family was originally from another country. **Expedition Tool: Charting Family** helps students document where their families originated even if it is only from another state.

- Immigration can be discussed as moving from one area or region to another, as well as from one country to another. In this way, students can recognize that everyone except Native Americans are considered immigrants to the United States. It is interesting for students to see the percentage of families that have lived in the same area for generations.

- Many students might not recognize their own family has traditions. It is helpful to make it clear that traditions are events that families do year after year. These can be things such as going to fireworks on the Fourth of July, camping every year at the end of school, having family reunions each year with relatives, or serving a specific food at a special time of year. Some of these traditions might have cultural origins, while the family might have created some. The role of family traditions can be discussed after the students have done their quickwrite. It is helpful to pre-identify some of the possible traditions based upon your knowledge of students' backgrounds.

- You might wish to have ESL students write their letter in their own language, read their letter so students can hear the language, and then work with a partner to verbally describe the tradition to the class.

Finding Your Roots

- It is helpful to have a world map to identify countries that students have in their cultural heritage.

Suggested Assessment

Use the Project Assessment Rubric or the following point system:

Team and class participation	15 points
Student quickwrite	15 points
Before You Go	25 points
Activity 1	35 points
Self-Assessment and Reflection	10 points

Extension Activities

- Students can illustrate their letters.
- Students can do research on cultural traditions in other countries.
- Students can bring in items that are used as part of their traditions and give presentations to the class.
- The class can celebrate a holiday using some of the traditions.

Common Core State Standards Connection

Writing: Production and Distribution of Writing

W.6.4, W.7.4, W.8.4. Produce clear and coherent writing in which the development, organization, and style are appropriate to task, purpose, and audience.

Writing: Research to Build and Present Knowledge

W.6.7, W.7.7. Conduct short research projects to answer a question, drawing on several sources....

W.8.7. Conduct short research projects to answer a question (including a self-generated question), drawing on several sources....

Language: Conventions of Standard English

L.6.2b, L.7.2b, L.8.2c. Spell correctly.

 163

Finding Your Roots

Answer Key

Check Yourself! Skill Check

1. Someone from another country might not be familiar with some words or expressions used. These should be either replaced with easier words or described fully. For those learning to read English, sentences should be simple, not overly complex with too many prepositional phrases.

2. Immigration is movement into a different area, region, or country one is not a native of in order to live.

3. A family tradition can be a religious practice, an event that recurs every year, or a special way that a family celebrates a holiday or an event.

4. Genealogy is a description of your family tree. It identifies your parents, grandparents, brothers and sisters, and other relatives. Some of these individuals might have grown up in other countries and in different cultures. Along with inheriting genetic traits from these individuals, you might also have inherited some family traditions that stem from these other cultures.

Finding Your Roots

Expedition Overview

Challenge
Here's your chance to explore your family's cultural roots! You will identify where your parents, grandparents, and great-grandparents lived. With your classmates, you will learn about traditions from different cultures. Then you will describe a family tradition to a pen pal from another country.

Objectives
- To explore genealogy and identify any cultural traditions your family celebrates
- To write a description of your tradition in a letter to a pen pal
- To use the writing process to create, edit, and revise your letter

Project Activities
Before You Go
- Family Heritage

Off You Go
- Activity 1: Holiday Traditions

Expedition Tools
- Charting Family
- Guide to Writing Letters
- Sample Letter

Other Materials Needed
- notebook
- pencil

Lingo to Learn—Terms to Know
- cultural heritage
- genealogy
- immigration
- traditions

Finding Your Roots

Expedition Overview

Helpful Web Resources

- Café Traditions
  www.cafetraditions.com

- History.com—Featured Topics: Holidays
  www.history.com/topics#all

- Museum of Science and Industry—Holiday Traditions
  www.msichicago.org/scrapbook/scrapbook_exhibits/catw2004/holiday_traditions.html

- Wikipedia—Cultural heritage
  http://en.wikipedia.org/wiki/Cultural_heritage

- Wikipedia—Family traditions
  http://en.wikipedia.org/wiki/Family_traditions

Finding Your Roots

Before You Go

Family Heritage

Goal:	To identify the cultural heritage of your family as well as the traditions associated with that heritage
Materials:	notebook, pencil
Tools:	Charting Family

Directions

Part 1: Family History

With the help of a relative, answer the questions below for your mother, father, and grandparents. Put your answers in the **Family History** table in the **Charting Family Expedition Tool.** You may add or delete columns or rows depending on the makeup of your family.

1. Has this person always lived in the state where he or she currently lives?

2. When did he or she come to this state?

3. From which state did he or she move?

4. Has this person always lived in the United States?

5. If not, when did he or she come to this country?

6. From which country did he or she move?

Part 2: Family Traditions

Complete the **Family Traditions** table in the **Expedition Tool.** In the first column, describe your family traditions. In the second column, tell where each tradition comes from.

Finding Your Roots

Expedition Tool

Charting Family
Family History

	Mother	Father	Grandmother (mother's mother)	Grandfather (mother's father)	Grandmother (father's mother)	Grandfather (father's father)
Always lived in current state?						
When came to this state						
State moved from						
Always lived in the United States?						
When came to this country						
Country moved from						

(continued)

Finding Your Roots

Expedition Tool

Family Traditions

Family tradition	State/country of origin

Finding Your Roots

Off You Go

Activity 1: Holiday Traditions

Goal:	To write a letter describing a holiday tradition in your family to someone from another culture
Materials:	notebook
Tools:	Guide to Writing Letters, Sample Letter

Directions

Part 1

1. In pairs, share family holiday traditions. Allow your partner to ask questions so you can clarify or expand the description of your tradition.

2. Read **Expedition Tool: Guide to Writing Letters.**

3. On a sheet of notebook paper, write two or three sentences describing the tradition you will write about in a letter to a pen pal in another country.

Part 2

1. Review **Expedition Tool: Sample Letter.** Note the different parts of the letter and the style it is written in.

2. What did the author use as a greeting?

   _____

3. What did the author use as the closing?

   _____

4. What does the author want to do as a next step?

   _____

   _____

5. Why did the author add extra details to the description of the family tradition?

   _____

   _____

   _____

(continued)

Finding Your Roots

Off You Go

6. Discuss your answers with a partner and then with the whole class.

7. On a separate sheet of paper, write a letter to a pen pal in another country that describes a family holiday tradition. Use the Expedition Tools to guide you.

8. Trade letters with a partner. Read each other's work, identifying any parts that might be confusing to a student in another country.

9. Revise your letter as needed.

10. Trade letters with a different partner. Proofread each other's work, correcting any mistakes in grammar, punctuation, or spelling.

11. Write a final draft of your letter and turn it in to your teacher.

Finding Your Roots

Expedition Tool

Guide to Writing Letters

- Write your name and address at the top of the letter. You can include your phone number and e-mail address if you like.
- Include the date.
- Write the name and address of the person receiving the letter.
- Use a greeting such as *Dear* or *To.*
- Use a block form. For each new paragraph, skip a line instead of indenting.
- Clearly organize your ideas. Open with an introductory paragraph summarizing why you are writing.
- In following paragraphs, give more detail to the ideas presented in the opening paragraph.
- In the closing paragraph, summarize your ideas again. If desired, mention actions such as getting together, speaking on the phone, or receiving a reply.
- After the closing paragraph, skip two lines and use a closing such as *Sincerely, Gratefully, Thank You,* and so forth. The closing is always capitalized.
- After the closing, skip three lines and type or print your name.
- Sign your name, putting your signature between the closing and your printed name.
- The abbreviation *cc:* stands for *carbon copy.* It is always lowercase. If you are sending other people a copy of the same letter, use this abbreviation and list those people's names.
- The abbreviation *encl:* stands for *enclosure.* It is always lowercase. If you are enclosing any attachments with your letter, include this abbreviation and write the name of the attachment.

© Walch Education

Finding Your Roots

Expedition Tool

Sample Letter

Jane Dorsey
32 Never Better Road
Neverland, MA 04237 | Your contact information |
jdorsey@neverland.org

November 17, 2012 | Date |

Pen Pal
Another City Road | Recipient's address |
Another Country, World XXVOC

Hello Pen Pal, | Greeting |

It is raining and colder today. We are preparing for our annual Thanksgiving celebration. In the United States, we have Thanksgiving in November. It is a holiday that celebrates our thanks for all we have. It occurs after the fall harvest from farms.

> The opening paragraph summarizes why you are writing.

At our home, we have our nearby relatives and friends over for a traditional turkey dinner. A turkey is a large bird that lives in the forests in the United States. Farmers also raise it. It can grow to be 25 pounds. It is usually baked for a long time in the oven.

> Paragraphs 2–6 give more details about what you mentioned in your introduction.

We have one special event other than the big meal. My grandmother's family from New England started the tradition. New England is the northeast corner of the United States. We have done this family tradition every year since we moved to New England. We could start the tradition again when we moved to New England because it was the first time we had a garden.

At the end of the harvest from the garden, we clean the garden. We pull out all the dead plants and place them in the center of the garden to dry. We also clean up the yard. We have many large maple trees, and all their leaves fall in October. Therefore, we rake the fallen leaves into a large pile by the garden to dry. We also trim the trees and shrubs, cutting off any dead or broken branches. We place some of these on the pile in the garden. We also have a special place we put the Christmas tree from the previous year to dry. We pull this out and place it on top of the pile. On Thanksgiving Day, my mother starts cooking

(continued)

Finding Your Roots

Expedition Tool

early in the morning. She bakes pies, fixes vegetables, and puts the turkey in the oven to bake. In the late morning, when the turkey is cooking, we all go out and light the burn pile to have what we call a bonfire. We put chairs around the fire to sit and warm ourselves throughout the day. We add logs from our winter wood supply throughout the day. For us, these activities mark the change in seasons. It is the end of the growing season and our time outside. It means the coming of a cold, snowy winter when we will spend most of our time inside.

I really like this holiday tradition. It is so much fun to poke at the fire and keep it burning all day. I like to go get more wood to put on the fire. As the sun begins to go down, it feels so good to sit close to the fire and feel its warmth. As it gets dark, I watch the flames flicker amongst the logs. We have eaten by then, and I feel so full from all the good food. If we are lucky, the stars come out, and we can see the sky full of the flickering lights. It is such a nice way to spend time with all our family and celebrate all the things we have—our health, the food, and a warm home.

Do you celebrate any type of harvest festival in your country? I would like to hear what you do to celebrate any holidays. Please write me and describe some of the things your family does together.

> The closing paragraph summarizes your ideas again. This is where you invite the recipient to reply to you.

With Interest,

> Closing remark. Skip three spaces before typing or printing your name. Then, sign your name in the space.

Jane Dorsey

> Closing signature

Jane Dorsey

Finding Your Roots

Check Yourself!

Skill Check

1. What should you remember to do when writing to a person from another culture?

   _____

   _____

   _____

2. What is immigration?

   _____

   _____

   _____

   _____

3. What is a family tradition?

   _____

   _____

   _____

4. What is the connection between genealogy and cultural heritage?

   _____

   _____

   _____

Finding Your Roots

Check Yourself!

Self-Assessment and Reflection

Before You Go

❑ I understand what genealogy is and can interview a relative to find our family history.

Off You Go

❑ I understand what a family tradition is.

❑ I can describe a family holiday tradition.

❑ I know how to write, edit, and revise a letter.

Do You Know?

❑ I can define the Lingo to Learn vocabulary terms for this project and give an example of each.

❑ I completed the Skill Check questions and carefully reviewed questions I did not answer correctly.

Reflection

1. What were the most challenging aspects of this project for you and why?

   _____

   _____

   _____

2. Which skills did this project help you develop?

   _____

   _____

   _____

3. If you did this project again, what might you do differently and why?

   _____

   _____

   _____

Class Ezine

Overview

Students will create content to be used in an online magazine (ezine) for their classmates and for youth who are new to the area. The ezine content will depict their favorite places to go and things to do in their community.

Time

Total time: 5 to 6 hours

- **Before You Go—Information Sources:** one class and 20 minutes of homework, pp. 185–190
- **Activity 1—Writing a News Article:** two classes and 40 minutes of homework, pp. 191–193
- **Activity 2—Magazine Extras:** one class and 20 minutes of homework, pp. 194–195
- **Activity 3—Making a Splash:** one class, pp. 196–197
- **Check Yourself! Skill Check** and **Self-Assessment and Reflection** worksheets: 30 minutes of class time or homework, pp. 198–199

Materials

- sample magazines
- notebook
- pencil
- digital camera (optional)

Skill Focus

- editing and revising writing
- evaluating media content
- journalism

Prior Knowledge

- using technology
- reviewing grammar and sentence structure

Team Formation

- Students work in pairs, as individuals, and as a whole class.

Lingo to Learn—Terms to Know

- **bio:** a short biographical description of an individual
- **feature article:** a more in-depth look at what's going on behind the news (versus a breaking story or hard news)

- **five *W*s and *H*:** who, what, where, when, why, and how; questions that a news story should answer
- **hook:** catchy part of the story opening or headline that readers remember and like the most
- **inverted pyramid:** common style of writing news in which the most important or interesting information is presented first
- **lede/lead:** first paragraph of a news story

Suggested Steps

Preparation

- Review all the materials and activities for the expedition. Note printables that you'll need to copy.
- Collect issues of local papers and magazines to analyze. Ask students to bring in one or two magazines from their home. Any school-appropriate topic will work.
- Contact your technology support to discuss placing the class ezine online.
- You could contact any real-estate agents who might be interested in knowing of this resource for new families moving into the area.
- You might also want to contact the administration and guidance office of the school to let them know about the project and its usefulness for students new to the area.
- It might be helpful to have the principal or guidance counselor speak to the class about the usefulness of the ezine.

Day 1

1. Describe the project. Students will write short and feature articles for a class ezine designed to provide other teens with information on fun things to do and places to go.

2. If possible, have the principal or guidance counselor speak to the class about the importance of this tool for new students to the area.

3. Distribute **Before You Go: Information Sources** (p. 185), along with **Expedition Tool: Magazine Content** (pp. 186–188) and **Expedition Tool: Your Class Ezine** (pp. 189–190). Review with students.

4. Have students work in pairs to analyze the format of at least two magazines using **Expedition Tool: Magazine Content** (pp. 186–188). They will identify feature articles, departments, and so forth. An example is provided.

5. Give students time to work in pairs to design a format of their class ezine.

6. Have the entire group share their ideas and come to an agreement on the format and title of the ezine.

Class Ezine

Homework

Students should identify a topic for one feature article and at least eight topics for short snapshots in their class ezine.

Day 2

1. Have students share their topic ideas with a partner. Direct each pair of students to select their favorite feature article idea and three short snapshot topics.

2. Pause to share ideas as a whole class.

3. Organize the list of topics into clusters of similar topics. For instance, there may be several restaurants, recreation ideas, etc.

4. Facilitate student decision-making about what the organizing ideas and subsequent topics will be.

5. Organize students into writing teams to work on sections of the ezine.

6. Distribute **Activity 1: Writing a News Article** (p. 191), along with **Expedition Tool: Writing Guidelines** (p. 192) and **Expedition Tool: Sample News Article** (p. 193).

7. Review the writing style necessary for journalism. Discuss how it is similar to and different from other genres of writing students have done.

8. Assign students to work in pairs to read the sample article and analyze the journalistic techniques.

9. Tell the writing teams to decide who will write which articles. Each student should write two short snapshots or one feature article.

Homework

Have students write their articles.

Day 3

1. Allow time for students to work in their teams and share their articles with a partner. In peer review, students review each other's work, keeping the key features of journalistic writing in mind.

2. Meet with each writing team to review their articles.

3. Have students revise their writing based on peer review.

Class Ezine

4. After students have revised their articles, direct them to find another student to proofread their work.

5. Distribute **Activity 2: Magazine Extras** (p. 192) and **Expedition Tool: Writing a Bio** (p. 193). Review with students.

Homework
Have students write a short bio as a contributor to the ezine.

Day 4

1. Have students get into their writing teams to share their bios and revise them as needed.

2. If possible, set up a process for taking a digital picture of each contributing author to accompany his or her bio.

3. Distribute **Activity 3: Making a Splash** (p. 194) and **Expedition Tool: Writing Headlines** (p. 195). Go over guidelines with students.

4. Have students work in their writing teams to write headlines for their articles. Students should review one another's work and revise as needed, then add the final headlines to their articles.

5. Place the class ezine online and make it available for others to review.

Final Day

1. Have students complete the **Check Yourself! Skill Check** questions (p. 196).

2. Check and review answers.

3. Have students complete the **Check Yourself! Self-Assessment and Reflection** worksheet (p. 197) and submit it (optional).

Class Ezine

Project Management Tips and Notes

- If students have not had much experience reading magazines or newspapers, it might be helpful to lead up to this project by having them read newspapers for a few weeks. A quick project is to have students bring in a news article (it can be off the Internet) with a short written summary each week. Students can share their article with a partner briefly at the beginning of class. The articles can be kept for other students to read during free time. This will acquaint students with format and headlines.

- If students are having a hard time listing ideas for the class ezine, it might be helpful for them to look at a local newspaper. See if it has a young adult section. It may already identify some of the types of activities that are attractive to teens.

Suggested Assessment

Use the Project Assessment Rubric or the following point system:

Team and class participation	15 points
Before You Go	15 points
Activity 1	35 points
Activity 2	15 points
Activity 3	15 points
Self-Assessment and Reflection	5 points

Extension Activities

- Students can create the online welcome page for their ezine.
- Students can program the Web site links.
- Students can illustrate their articles.
- Students can create a Web calendar of events for teens.

Common Core State Standards Connection

Writing: Text Types and Purposes

W.6.2, W.7.2, W.8.2. Write informative/explanatory texts to examine a topic and convey ideas, concepts, and information through the selection, organization, and analysis of relevant content.

   d.   Use precise language and domain-specific vocabulary to inform about or explain the topic.

Class Ezine

Writing: Production and Distribution of Writing

W.6.4, W.7.4, W.8.4. Produce clear and coherent writing in which the development, organization, and style are appropriate to task, purpose, and audience.

W.6.5. With some guidance and support from peers and adults, develop and strengthen writing as needed by planning, revising, editing, rewriting, or trying a new approach.

W.6.6. Use technology, including the Internet, to produce and publish writing as well as to interact and collaborate with others….

Writing: Research to Build and Present Knowledge

W.6.8. Gather relevant information from multiple print and digital sources … and quote or paraphrase the data and conclusions of others while avoiding plagiarism….

W.7.8, W.8.8. Gather relevant information from multiple print and digital sources, using search terms effectively … and quote or paraphrase the data and conclusions of others while avoiding plagiarism….

Writing: Range of Writing

W.6.10, W.7.10, W.8.10. Write routinely over extended time frames (time for research, reflection, and revision) and shorter time frames (a single sitting or a day or two) for a range of discipline-specific tasks, purposes, and audiences.

Answer Key

Check Yourself! Skill Check

1. Journalism is the genre of writing used in newspapers and magazines.

2. Journalistic articles should answer the five *W*'s and *H*—who, what, when, where, why, and how. Information should be in an inverted triangle format. The most important information should be at the top of the article, and the least important information at the end.

3. Headlines and the lead in an opening paragraph can be used as hooks to catch the reader's attention and encourage him or her to continue reading the article.

4. When inviting a reader into a text, an author increases a reader's interest in the text by giving him or her clear, active descriptions that illustrate a place or person.

5. Using a direct quote from an individual appeals to the reader and makes the article more believable.

Class Ezine

Expedition Overview

Challenge

Start the presses! Here's your chance to create an online magazine, an ezine, with your class. You will highlight activities in your community and provide a summary for other young people of places to go and things to do.

Objectives

- To learn about the format of a magazine
- To learn about the genre of journalism
- To identify and create content for an ezine

Project Activities

Before You Go

- Information Sources

Off You Go

- Activity 1: Writing a News Article
- Activity 2: Magazine Extras
- Activity 3: Making a Splash

Expedition Tools

- Magazine Content
- Your Class Ezine
- Writing Guidelines
- Sample News Article
- Writing a Bio
- Writing Headlines

Other Materials Needed

- sample magazines
- notebook
- pencil
- digital camera (optional)

Class Ezine

Expedition Overview

Lingo to Learn—Terms to Know
- bio
- feature article
- five *W*'s and *H*
- hook
- inverted pyramid
- lede/lead

Helpful Web Resources
- Enchanted Learning—Make a Classroom Newspaper
  www.enchantedlearning.com/newspaper

- Scholastic (News Writing)—Step 3: Writing Techniques
  http://teacher.scholastic.com/writewit/news/step3.htm

- Wikipedia—Ezine (Online magazine)
  http://en.wikipedia.org/wiki/Ezine

- Wikipedia—Journalism
  http://en.wikipedia.org/wiki/Journalism

Class Ezine

Before You Go

Information Sources

Goal:	To learn about the format of magazines
Materials:	sample magazines, notebook, pencil
Tools:	Magazine Content, Your Class Ezine

Directions

Magazines contain articles of varying length on a variety of topics. All of the articles are focused on one or two themes. Your ezine will highlight activities in your community for young people. It will describe places to go and things to do. It's up to you and your writing team to organize the content. You will need to find suitable topics for longer articles and decide what will be written in short snapshot articles.

1. With a partner, analyze at least two magazines. Look at the example magazine content analysis contained in **Expedition Tool: Magazine Content.** Then complete your own magazine content analysis.

2. Work in pairs to create a table of contents for your class ezine. Decide on the type of articles you will include, their length, and the numbers of each type.

3. Share your list with the class. Together, your class will decide what the ezine format will be using the **Your Class Ezine Expedition Tool.**

4. Identify one topic for a feature article and at least eight topics for short snapshots for your magazine.

5. Share your list of topics with a partner.

6. From both of your lists, select one feature article and three short snapshot ideas.

7. Be prepared to work with your class to turn everyone's ideas into the class ezine.

Class Ezine

Expedition Tool

Magazine Content
Example: Magazine Content Analysis
Magazine: *Orion*

Type of article	Length of article	Topics	Number of similar articles
Features	6–8 pages	Plastic in the environment Working from home Life of Inuits	7
Departments	1–2 pages with many subheadings and short articles	Letters to the editor Editorials Book reviews Health and the environment Grassroots network	5
Columns	2 pages	Thoreau Writing	2
Poems	Less than 1 page	Life Fish Concerns	4

(continued)

Class Ezine

Expedition Tool

Magazine Content Analysis

1. Magazine: _____

Type of article	Length of article	Topics	Number of similar articles

(continued)

Class Ezine

Expedition Tool

2. Magazine: _____

Type of article	Length of article	Topics	Number of similar articles

Class Ezine

Expedition Tool

Your Class Ezine
Proposed Ezine Format

Class ezine title: _____

Type of article	Length of article	Number of similar articles

(continued)

Class Ezine

Expedition Tool

Ezine Topics

Feature article topic:

_____

_____

_____

_____

Short snapshot article topics:

1. _____

_____

2. _____

_____

3. _____

_____

4. _____

_____

5. _____

_____

6. _____

_____

7. _____

_____

8. _____

_____

Class Ezine

Off You Go

Activity 1: Writing a News Article

Goal:	To learn about writing news articles
Materials:	pencil, notebook
Tools:	Writing Guidelines, Sample News Article

Directions

1. Review **Expedition Tool: Writing Guidelines.**

2. With a partner, read **Expedition Tool: Sample News Article** on carbon footprints. Analyze how the author did and did not follow the proper guidelines for writing news articles.

3. With your writing team, decide who will write which articles. Each student should write two short snapshots or one feature article.

4. On a separate sheet of paper, write the articles assigned to you by your team. Make sure you follow the guidelines for writing news articles.

5. Share your article(s) with a partner.

6. Revise your article based on your partner's comments. Then turn it in according to your teacher's instructions.

Class Ezine

Expedition Tool

Writing Guidelines

- When you write a news article, answer the 5 *W*s and *H* questions: who, what, when, where, why, and how.
- Write the most important information in the first paragraph. Add details in the supporting paragraphs. Write about the least important information at the end of the article. This organizational style is called an inverted triangle. All the most important information is a broad line at the top—the 5 *W*s and *H* of the lead paragraph at the beginning. The least important information is the small tip, in this case at the bottom of the article.

Most Important

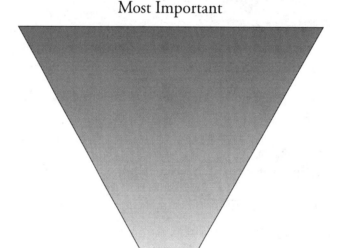

Least Important

- Write an attention-getting first and second sentence in your opening paragraph (a lead or lede—both spellings are pronounced *leed*). This is also called a hook—to "catch" the reader's interest.
- Be clear and brief. Use simple sentences. Do not include any unnecessary information. Be specific with important details.
- Use strong words and an active voice.
- Be sure you are fair. Do not express an opinion unless it is an editorial. Otherwise, the article should present both sides of any issue.
- Add interest by using quotations. Having a real person discuss what you are writing about adds appeal for the reader.
- Be sure to check your facts.

Expedition Tool

Sample News Article

Are You Leaving a Carbon Footprint? How to Hide Your Tracks

ATLANTA, GA (May 2, 2009)—Whether you are making a cup of coffee, driving to the grocery store, mowing the yard, taking a shower, or even opening the refrigerator door, you are leaving a trail that tells a lot about your life.

Just about all activities that use energy to almost any degree are creating individual carbon footprints.

A carbon footprint is a measure of the amount of carbon dioxide and other greenhouse gases that are released into the atmosphere as people go about their routine daily activities.

By making small and seemingly insignificant changes in daily routines, people can not only reduce the size of their carbon footprint, but also realize significant savings in their energy costs.

There are a number of Web sites that have calculators that enable people to determine how much energy they consume and suggestions on how to reduce the size of their carbon footprint. Some suggestions involve significant lifestyle changes, ranging from trading in an SUV for a hybrid or riding a bicycle to work. Others are more practical and simple, such as turning the home thermostat down a degree or two.

Here are some easy tips that most people can follow without too much effort:

- Air conditioning and heating: By simply turning the air conditioning up a couple of degrees in the summer and the heating systems down in the winter, a consumer can save several hundred dollars.
- Shower: Install a low-flow shower head and take shorter showers to reduce the amount of water used. Taking a shower instead of a bath saves considerable amounts of water.

- Refrigerator: Place the refrigerator in a cool spot. Don't place hot food inside. For greater efficiency, keep coils clean and defrost it on a regular basis if necessary.
- Electronic devices: Unplug those that aren't being used, such as cell-phone chargers, hair dryers, coffee pots, computers, etc. as they use electricity just by being plugged in.
- Hot-water heater: Reducing the temperature of a hot-water heater from 140 degrees F to 120 degrees F not only saves money but may prevent scalding. Insulate the hot-water heater to save even more.
- Clothes washer: Wash clothes in cold water. Many detergents are designed for this purpose. Hot water is only necessary for extremely dirty or greasy items.
- Clothes dryer, oven, and dishwasher: Wait until the sun goes down in the summer months to run these appliances so they don't put more strain on the air conditioner. In the winter months, run them when the house is the coolest.

Consumers can access the Energy Wizard at www.EnergyWizard.info to read about a range of topics from conservation and new technologies to generators and tax incentives; ask energy related questions; or read the latest Energy Wizard columns.

David Scott
(EnergyWizard@EnergyWizard.info)
Energy Wizard

From Press Releases Online:
http://pressreleasesonline.biz/pr/Want_to_Hide_Your_Carbon_Footprint.php

Class Ezine

Off You Go

Activity 2: Magazine Extras

Goal:	To learn how to write a short biography, or bio, as a contributing author to the class ezine
Materials:	magazines, notebook, digital camera (optional)
Tool:	Writing a Bio

Directions

1. Review **Expedition Tool: Writing a Bio.**

2. Using the magazines you have on hand, look for short biographies, or bios, of the contributing authors. *Hint:* Sometimes these are in a special section of the magazine, and sometimes the information is placed at the end of each article.

3. In the space below or on a separate sheet of paper, write a short bio on yourself. Follow the guidelines in the Expedition Tool.

4. Share your bio with other students on your team. Receive feedback and revise as needed.

5. If possible, have your picture taken to accompany your bio.

My Bio

_____

_____

_____

_____

_____

_____

_____

_____

_____

_____

_____

Class Ezine

Expedition Tool

Writing a Bio

- Start the paragraph with your name. Write in the third person, as though someone else is talking abut you.
- Identify any experience that makes you a believable author of the article. What is your background? What experience do you have that leads you to know about the topic?
- Note where you live. Include a sentence about your family.

Example:

John Doe is a sixth-grade student who loves to skateboard. He has been riding a long board for the past two years. He competed in the Park Playoff skateboard competition and won second place. John lives with his two brothers and parents in My Town, USA.

Class Ezine

Off You Go

Activity 3: Making a Splash

Goal:	To learn to write headlines for news articles
Materials:	pencil, notebook
Tool:	Writing Headlines

Directions

1. Review **Expedition Tool: Writing Headlines.**

2. With a partner, write the headlines for your news articles. Be sure to follow the guidelines in the Expedition Tool.

_____

_____

_____

3. Share your headlines with the other students on your team.

4. Receive feedback and revise as needed. Write your final headlines below. Then add them at the top of your news articles.

_____

_____

_____

Class Ezine

Expedition Tool

Writing Headlines

- Write one sentence that summarizes the article.
- Look for key nouns in your sentence or in the article itself that tell it all.
- Add a strong, active verb in present tense.
- Add only words that clarify and sharpen the statement. Be sure they are common, colorful, and specific words.
- Make the reader curious enough to read the story, but be sure the headline leads to the story.
- Make sure the headline matches the lead.
- Be careful of words with two meanings.
- Do not use a name unless it is immediately recognizable by the reader.

Class Ezine

Check Yourself!

Skill Check

1. What is journalism?

   _____

   _____

   _____

2. What are some important guidelines to remember when writing for newspapers and magazines?

   _____

   _____

   _____

   _____

3. When writing a news article, what are some tools for catching a reader's attention?

   _____

   _____

   _____

   _____

4. What is meant by inviting the reader into a story?

   _____

   _____

   _____

   _____

5. Why is it helpful to use quotations in a news article?

   _____

   _____

   _____

Class Ezine

Check Yourself!

Self-Assessment and Reflection

Before You Go
- ❑ I know how to analyze a magazine and determine its format.

Off You Go
- ❑ I know how to write a news article for a magazine.
- ❑ I can analyze a news article to see if it meets stated guidelines.
- ❑ I can write a bio to summarize who I am and why I am qualified to write a story.
- ❑ I can write headlines for my news articles.
- ❑ I understand how to review and edit my writing.

Do You Know?
- ❑ I can define the Lingo to Learn vocabulary terms for this project and give an example of each.
- ❑ I completed the Skill Check questions and carefully reviewed questions I did not answer correctly.

Reflection

1. What were the most challenging aspects of this project for you and why?

   _____

   _____

   _____

2. Which skills did this project help you develop?

   _____

   _____

   _____

3. If you did this project again, what might you do differently and why?

   _____

   _____

   _____

You're the Playwright

Overview

Students learn about plays. They explore the use of settings and dialogue to portray characters in a given time and place. Students write their own plays that depict their community 100 years in the future and illustrate positive changes that have occurred.

Time

Total time: 10 to 11 hours

- **Before You Go—Setting the Scene:** one class and 2 hours of homework, pp. 209–221
- **Activity 1—Into the Future:** one class and 30 minutes of homework, pp. 222–225
- **Activity 2—Dialogue:** one class and 30 minutes of homework, pp. 226–227
- **Activity 3—Writing Your Play:** four classes and 60 minutes of homework, pp. 228–230
- **Check Yourself! Skill Check** and **Self-Assessment and Reflection** worksheets: 30 minutes of class time or homework, pp. 231–232

Materials

- notebook
- pencil
- items as props
- clothing for costumes
- furniture or items for scenery

Skill Focus

- character
- editing and revising writing
- analyzing story/presentation structure
- oral-presentation skills

Prior Knowledge

- peer editing

Team Formation

- Students work in pairs, as individuals, and as a whole class.

You're the Playwright

Lingo to Learn—Terms to Know

- **act:** one section of a play that contains one part of the story, like a chapter of a book
- **character:** an individual in a play
- **characterization:** the method a writer uses to develop a character
- **dialogue:** conversation between two or more characters in a play
- **props:** items used by the performers during a play
- **scene:** one physical setting at a given time in a play that is displayed with furniture, structures, and backdrops
- **setting:** the time, place, and environment in which a story unfolds

Suggested Steps

Preparation

- Review all the materials and activities for the expedition. Note printables that you'll need to copy.
- Select a one-act or short play for all students to read and analyze.
- If a drama coach or teacher is in your school, you might wish to ask him or her to work with students on their plays and discuss the tool of dialogue to convey character.
- If you intend to have students perform for the school or the community, schedule the presentation.
- If desired, ask town-council members to attend the presentation and respond to students' portrayals of a future community.

Day 1

1. Describe the project. Students will learn about plays in preparation for writing their own short play. The play will depict their town in the idealized future. Students will select a place within their town that they will portray as having changed for the better. The audience will guess where the play takes place in their community, how it has changed for the better, and describe the personalities of the characters depicted.

2. Distribute **Before You Go: Setting the Scene** (p. 209), along with **Expedition Tool: How Dramatic** (pp. 210–218) and **Expedition Tool: Taking Notes** (pp. 219–221).

3. Review the definitions in Part 1 of **Expedition Tool: How Dramatic.**

4. Review the scene description and list of characters from the play excerpt in Part 2 of the Expedition Tool. Assign a student to read each character's part.

5. Read aloud a portion of the dialogue with the students.

6. As they read their parts, project a copy of the graphic organizer for note-taking. Stop periodically, or ask students to raise their hands when they can add something to the organizer.

You're the Playwright

7. When you complete reading the play, discuss the notes taken. Confirm students' ideas about settings, characters, and dialogue.

8. Assign students the play, or the portion of a play, that you have selected for them to read.

9. Ask students to use their copy of the graphic organizer to take notes while they are reading.

Homework

Have students read the assigned play and take notes.

Day 2

1. Have students work in pairs to share their notes identifying the personalities of the characters they discovered through the dialogue, as well as the specifics of the settings.

2. Discuss ideas as a whole class.

3. Distribute **Activity 1: Into the Future** (p. 222) and **Expedition Tool: Sample Settings** (pp. 223–225).

4. Discuss the different settings as a class.

Homework

Have students describe the setting for their play, which will take place somewhere in the community 100 years in the future. Remind students that they will need to choose a real place in the community that they envision changing for the better.

Day 3

1. In pairs, students share their settings. Ask them to choose one setting. Students will work together to create a play using this setting.

2. Distribute **Activity 2: Dialogue** (p. 226) and **Expedition Tool: Revealing Your Character** (p. 227).

3. As a class, create two characters and decide their personalities.

4. Assign pairs to create a dialogue that reveals each character's traits.

5. Invite pairs to read their dialogues. Ask them to explain what they did to reveal each character's traits.

You're the Playwright

6. Ask the student audience for positive, constructive comments.

7. Discuss the use of props and costumes in plays. Ask students if there could have been a prop or costume used in any of the dialogues that would have helped convey the personalities of the characters.

8. Distribute **Activity 3: Writing Your Play** (p. 228) and **Expedition Tool: All the Details** (pp. 229–230).

Homework

Have students begin work on their plays.

Day 4

1. Give student pairs time to continue work on their plays.

2. Instruct students to be descriptive when writing about the setting, characters, and delivery of dialogue.

3. Make students aware that they will not be able to use very many pieces of furniture or physical structures. If these items are part of the scene, they will need to be described by the characters.

4. Set down guidelines for both props and costumes. There should be no elaborate costumes. Students should just use conventional clothing. Props can be things from around the house or items made out of cardboard.

Homework

Students should continue to work on their plays.

Day 5

1. Meet with each pair of students to review their progress.

2. Allow students time to keep writing.

3. Support pairs as they finalize their props, costumes, and sets for their dialogue.

Homework

Students should practice the play in preparation for sharing with the class.

Day 6

1. Invite pairs to present their play with props, costumes, and setting.

2. Instruct the audience to write a review on an index card that identifies where the play took place and two personality traits for each character.

3. When everyone has completed their presentations, give the review cards to the actors and actresses. Each pair counts how many audience members were correct.

4. Assign pairs with the fewest "correct" cards to revise their work.

5. If possible, host a performance for other students in the school or the community.

Final Day

1. Have students complete the **Check Yourself! Skill Check** questions (p. 231).

2. Check and review answers.

3. Have students complete the **Check Yourself! Self-Assessment and Reflection** worksheet (p. 232) and submit it (optional).

Project Management Tips and Notes

- The focus of this project should be on the use of dialogue to convey place and characters. From the beginning, explain the restrictions on the settings, props, and costumes. These will need to be very simple to assure all students are given an equal chance at focusing on the use of dialogue, not setting or props, for conveying the place and characters.

- If possible, after the performances, have a panel of the actors and actresses. Ask them about the future they portrayed. Have them discuss what they think would be improvements to the community and why they chose their spots and ideas to focus upon. If possible, have town council members attend and respond to the students' portrayals.

- Some students might have difficulty developing dialogue. They might think it has to be formal, similar to that in plays they have read. Share with them some contemporary plays that have vernacular in the dialogue. Set boundaries on the type of language that can be used, but convey to them that it can be a dialogue between people who are exactly like them. However, in this circumstance, they will need to convey more about who they are and what a change for the better would be in their community.

- If students have not had much exposure to plays, you could obtain a recording of a play for them to watch. You can also discuss the similarities and differences among plays, television shows, and movies. Some key differences students might recognize are the briefness of dialogue and the limited settings in plays versus in television shows or movies.

You're the Playwright

Suggested Assessment

Use the Project Assessment Rubric or the following point system:

Team and class participation	10 points
Before You Go	10 points
Activity 1	20 points
Activity 2	15 points
Activity 3	20 points
Student performance	20 points
Self-Assessment and Reflection	5 points

Extension Activities

- Students can write longer plays or include more characters.
- Students can create more elaborate scenery or costumes and perform for the community.
- Students can prepare to lead the discussion on characters and setting for the play the class read.
- Students can read another play and act out a portion in class, leading a discussion on the characters and setting.

Common Core State Standards Connection

Reading—Literature: Key Ideas and Details

RL.8.2. Determine a theme or central idea of a text and analyze its development over the course of the text, including its relationship to the characters, setting, and plot….

RL.6.3. Describe how a particular story's or drama's plot unfolds in a series of episodes as well as how the characters respond or change as the plot moves toward a resolution.

RL.7.3. Analyze how particular elements of a story or drama interact (e.g., how setting shapes the characters or plot).

RL.8.3. Analyze how particular lines of dialogue or incidents in a story or drama propel the action, reveal aspects of a character, or provoke a decision.

Reading—Literature: Craft and Structure

RL.6.5. Analyze how a particular sentence, chapter, scene, or stanza fits into the overall structure of a text and contributes to the development of the theme, setting, or plot.

You're the Playwright

Writing: Production and Distribution of Writing

W.6.4, W.7.4, W.8.4. Produce clear and coherent writing in which the development, organization, and style are appropriate to task, purpose, and audience.

Speaking and Listening: Presentation of Knowledge and Ideas

SL.6.6, SL.7.6, SL.8.6. Adapt speech to a variety of contexts and tasks, demonstrating command of formal English when indicated or appropriate.

Language: Conventions of Standard English

L.6.1, L.7.1, L.8.1. Demonstrate command of the conventions of standard English grammar and usage when writing or speaking.

Language: Knowledge of Language

L.6.3, L.7.3, L.8.3. Use knowledge of language and its conventions when writing, speaking, reading, or listening.

Language: Vocabulary Acquisition and Use

L.6.6, L.7.6, L.8.6. Acquire and use accurately grade-appropriate general academic and domain-specific words and phrases; gather vocabulary knowledge when considering a word or phrase important to comprehension or expression.

Answer Key
Check Yourself! Skill Check

1. A play is divided into acts and scenes. The acts are the larger part of the plot. They provide a break between major events, much like chapters in a book. A scene is a subset of an act. It is the dialogue or action that occurs within one physical setting in a play.

2. Props are items that are used to depict the play. They are usually used by the performers. Settings are the places and times in which the play occurs. Scenery consists of large pieces of furniture or backdrops that portray the place where the story is occurring.

3. A character is a person within a play. A characterization is developed when the personality of the character is evidenced through the actions and dialogue of the character.

4. Dialogue is conversation between two or more characters in a play.

You're the Playwright

Expedition Overview

Challenge

Here's your chance to add some drama to your life! In this Expedition, you will write a one-scene play that takes place in your community 100 years in the future. You will choose a place and portray it as having changed for the better. Your play will include a dialogue that will help the audience determine where the play takes place, how the place has changed for the better, and what the characters' personalities are.

Objectives

- To read a play and understand the development and use of settings and characters in the drama
- To create a setting of an improved future community
- To write a play that includes settings and characters
- To select simple props, costumes, and scenery to present the play

Project Activities

Before You Go
- Setting the Scene

Off You Go
- Activity 1: Into the Future
- Activity 2: Dialogue
- Activity 3: Writing Your Play

Expedition Tools
- How Dramatic
- Taking Notes
- Sample Settings
- Revealing Your Character
- All the Details

Other Materials Needed
- notebook
- pencil
- items as props
- clothing for costumes
- furniture or items for scenery

You're the Playwright

Expedition Overview

Lingo to Learn—Terms to Know
- act
- character
- characterization
- dialogue
- props
- scene
- setting

Helpful Web Resources
- The Kennedy Center—Arena Stage's Student Ten-Minute Plays
  www.kennedy-center.org/explorer/artists/?entity_id=11433&source_type=B
- One-Act-Plays.com
  http://one-act-plays.com
- Philadelphia Young Playwrights
  www.phillyyoungplaywrights.org
- SpokesmanReview.com—Student playwrights create depth
  www.spokesmanreview.com/blogs/video/archive.asp?postID=378

You're the Playwright

Before You Go

Setting the Scene

Goal:	To learn about plays
Materials:	notebook and pencil
Tools:	How Dramatic, Taking Notes

Directions

1. Read Part 1 of **Expedition Tool: How Dramatic** and review the definitions.

2. Look at the beginning of Part 2 of the Expedition Tool. Read the scene description and review the list of characters.

3. Read aloud a portion of the dialogue according to your teacher's instructions.

4. With the class, make observations about setting, characters, and props.

5. Read a play assigned to you by your teacher. Use **Expedition Tool: Taking Notes** to record your observations about the settings, characters, and props.

6. Prepare to share your notes with the class.

You're the Playwright

Expedition Tool

How Dramatic

Part 1: Glossary

- **act:** one section of a play that contains one part of the story, like a chapter of a book
- **character:** an individual in a play
- **characterization:** the method a writer uses to develop a character
- **dialogue:** conversation between two or more characters in a play
- **props:** items used by the performers during a play
- **scene:** one physical setting at a given time in a play that is displayed with furniture, structures, and backdrops
- **setting:** the time, place, and environment in which a story unfolds

Part 2: Excerpt

THE IMPORTANCE OF BEING EARNEST
A Trivial Comedy for Serious People
by Oscar Wilde

<u>Characters</u>

John Worthing, J.P.
Algernon Moncrieff
Rev. Canon Chasuble, D.D.
Merriman, Butler
Lane, Manservant
Lady Bracknell
Hon. Gwendolen Fairfax
Cecily Cardew
Miss Prism, Governess

THE SCENES OF THE PLAY

ACT I. Algernon Moncrieff's Flat in Half-Moon Street, London.

ACT II. The Garden at the Manor House, Woolton.

ACT III. Drawing-Room at the Manor House, Woolton.

TIME: late 1800s, England

(continued)

You're the Playwright

Expedition Tool

FIRST ACT

SCENE

Morning-room in Algernon's flat in Half-Moon Street. The room is luxuriously and artistically furnished. The sound of a piano is heard in the adjoining room.

[**Lane** is arranging afternoon tea on the table, and after the music has ceased, **Algernon** enters.]

ALGERNON: Did you hear what I was playing, Lane?

LANE: I didn't think it polite to listen, sir.

ALGERNON: I'm sorry for that, for your sake. I don't play accurately—any one can play accurately—but I play with wonderful expression. As far as the piano is concerned, sentiment is my forte. I keep science for Life.

LANE: Yes, sir.

ALGERNON: And, speaking of the science of Life, have you got the cucumber sandwiches cut for Lady Bracknell?

LANE: Yes, sir. [Hands them on a salver.]

ALGERNON: [Inspects them, takes two, and sits down on the sofa.] Oh! . . . by the way, Lane, I see from your book that on Thursday night, when Lord Shoreman and Mr. Worthing were dining with me, eight bottles of champagne are entered as having been consumed.

LANE: Yes, sir; eight bottles and a pint.

ALGERNON: Why is it that at a bachelor's establishment the servants invariably drink the champagne? I ask merely for information.

LANE: I attribute it to the superior quality of the wine, sir. I have often observed that in married households the champagne is rarely of a first-rate brand.

ALGERNON: Good heavens! Is marriage so demoralising as that?

LANE: I believe it *is* a very pleasant state, sir. I have had very little experience of it myself up to the present. I have only been married once. That was in consequence of a misunderstanding between myself and a young person.

ALGERNON: [Languidly.] I don't know that I am much interested in your family life, Lane.

LANE: No, sir; it is not a very interesting subject. I never think of it myself.

(*continued*)

You're the Playwright

Expedition Tool

ALGERNON: Very natural, I am sure. That will do, Lane, thank you.

LANE: Thank you, sir. [**Lane** goes out.]

ALGERNON: Lane's views on marriage seem somewhat lax. Really, if the lower orders don't set us a good example, what on earth is the use of them? They seem, as a class, to have absolutely no sense of moral responsibility.

[Enter **LANE**:]

LANE: Mr. Ernest Worthing.

[Enter **JACK**:]

[**Lane** goes out.]

ALGERNON: How are you, my dear Ernest? What brings you up to town?

JACK: Oh, pleasure, pleasure! What else should bring one anywhere? Eating as usual, I see, Algy!

ALGERNON: [Stiffly.] I believe it is customary in good society to take some slight refreshment at five o'clock. Where have you been since last Thursday?

JACK: [Sitting down on the sofa.] In the country.

ALGERNON: What on earth do you do there?

JACK: [Pulling off his gloves.] When one is in town one amuses oneself. When one is in the country one amuses other people. It is excessively boring.

ALGERNON: And who are the people you amuse?

JACK: [Airily.] Oh, neighbours, neighbours.

ALGERNON: Got nice neighbours in your part of Shropshire?

JACK: Perfectly horrid! Never speak to one of them.

ALGERNON: How immensely you must amuse them! [Goes over and takes sandwich.] By the way, Shropshire is your county, is it not?

JACK: Eh? Shropshire? Yes, of course. Hallo! Why all these cups? Why cucumber sandwiches? Why such reckless extravagance in one so young? Who is coming to tea?

ALGERNON: Oh! merely Aunt Augusta and Gwendolen.

JACK: How perfectly delightful!

(continued)

You're the Playwright

Expedition Tool

ALGERNON: Yes, that is all very well; but I am afraid Aunt Augusta won't quite approve of your being here.

JACK: May I ask why?

ALGERNON: My dear fellow, the way you flirt with Gwendolen is perfectly disgraceful. It is almost as bad as the way Gwendolen flirts with you.

JACK: I am in love with Gwendolen. I have come up to town expressly to propose to her.

ALGERNON: I thought you had come up for pleasure? . . . I call that business.

JACK: How utterly unromantic you are!

ALGERNON: I really don't see anything romantic in proposing. It is very romantic to be in love. But there is nothing romantic about a definite proposal. Why, one may be accepted. One usually is, I believe. Then the excitement is all over. The very essence of romance is uncertainty. If ever I get married, I'll certainly try to forget the fact.

JACK: I have no doubt about that, dear Algy. The Divorce Court was specially invented for people whose memories are so curiously constituted.

ALGERNON: Oh! there is no use speculating on that subject. Divorces are made in Heaven—[**Jack** puts out his hand to take a sandwich. **Algernon** at once interferes.] Please don't touch the cucumber sandwiches. They are ordered specially for Aunt Augusta. [Takes one and eats it.]

JACK: Well, you have been eating them all the time.

ALGERNON: That is quite a different matter. She is my aunt. [Takes plate from below.] Have some bread and butter. The bread and butter is for Gwendolen. Gwendolen is devoted to bread and butter.

JACK: [Advancing to table and helping himself.] And very good bread and butter it is too.

ALGERNON: Well, my dear fellow, you need not eat as if you were going to eat it all. You behave as if you were married to her already. You are not married to her already, and I don't think you ever will be.

JACK: Why on earth do you say that?

ALGERNON: Well, in the first place girls never marry the men they flirt with. Girls don't think it right.

JACK: Oh, that is nonsense!

(continued)

You're the Playwright

Expedition Tool

ALGERNON: It isn't. It is a great truth. It accounts for the extraordinary number of bachelors that one sees all over the place. In the second place, I don't give my consent.

JACK: Your consent!

ALGERNON: My dear fellow, Gwendolen is my first cousin. And before I allow you to marry her, you will have to clear up the whole question of Cecily. [Rings bell.]

JACK: Cecily! What on earth do you mean? What do you mean, Algy, by Cecily! I don't know any one of the name of Cecily.

[Enter **LANE**:]

ALGERNON: Bring me that cigarette case Mr. Worthing left in the smoking-room the last time he dined here.

LANE: Yes, sir. [**Lane** goes out.]

JACK: Do you mean to say you have had my cigarette case all this time? I wish to goodness you had let me know. I have been writing frantic letters to Scotland Yard about it. I was very nearly offering a large reward.

ALGERNON: Well, I wish you would offer one. I happen to be more than usually hard up.

JACK: There is no good offering a large reward now that the thing is found.

[Enter **Lane** with the cigarette case on a salver. **Algernon** takes it at once. **Lane** goes out.]

ALGERNON: I think that is rather mean of you, Ernest, I must say. [Opens case and examines it.] However, it makes no matter, for, now that I look at the inscription inside, I find that the thing isn't yours after all.

JACK: Of course it's mine. [Moving to him.] You have seen me with it a hundred times, and you have no right whatsoever to read what is written inside. It is a very ungentlemanly thing to read a private cigarette case.

ALGERNON: Oh! it is absurd to have a hard and fast rule about what one should read and what one shouldn't. More than half of modern culture depends on what one shouldn't read.

JACK: I am quite aware of the fact, and I don't propose to discuss modern culture. It isn't the sort of thing one should talk of in private. I simply want my cigarette case back.

ALGERNON: Yes; but this isn't your cigarette case. This cigarette case is a present from some one of the name of Cecily, and you said you didn't know any one of that name.

JACK: Well, if you want to know, Cecily happens to be my aunt.

(continued)

You're the Playwright

Expedition Tool

ALGERNON: Your aunt!

JACK: Yes. Charming old lady she is, too. Lives at Tunbridge Wells. Just give it back to me, Algy.

ALGERNON: [Retreating to back of sofa.] But why does she call herself little Cecily if she is your aunt and lives at Tunbridge Wells? [Reading.] 'From little Cecily with her fondest love.'

JACK: [Moving to sofa and kneeling upon it.] My dear fellow, what on earth is there in that? Some aunts are tall, some aunts are not tall. That is a matter that surely an aunt may be allowed to decide for herself. You seem to think that every aunt should be exactly like your aunt! That is absurd! For Heaven's sake give me back my cigarette case. [Follows **Algernon** round the room.]

ALGERNON: Yes. But why does your aunt call you her uncle? 'From little Cecily, with her fondest love to her dear Uncle JACK:' There is no objection, I admit, to an aunt being a small aunt, but why an aunt, no matter what her size may be, should call her own nephew her uncle, I can't quite make out. Besides, your name isn't Jack at all; it is Ernest.

JACK: It isn't Ernest; it's JACK.

ALGERNON: You have always told me it was Ernest. I have introduced you to every one as Ernest. You answer to the name of Ernest. You look as if your name was Ernest. You are the most earnest-looking person I ever saw in my life. It is perfectly absurd your saying that your name isn't Ernest. It's on your cards. Here is one of them. [Taking it from case.] 'Mr. Ernest Worthing, B. 4, The Albany.' I'll keep this as a proof that your name is Ernest if ever you attempt to deny it to me, or to Gwendolen, or to any one else. [Puts the card in his pocket.]

JACK: Well, my name is Ernest in town and Jack in the country, and the cigarette case was given to me in the country.

ALGERNON: Yes, but that does not account for the fact that your small Aunt Cecily, who lives at Tunbridge Wells, calls you her dear uncle. Come, old boy, you had much better have the thing out at once.

JACK: My dear Algy, you talk exactly as if you were a dentist. It is very vulgar to talk like a dentist when one isn't a dentist. It produces a false impression.

ALGERNON: Well, that is exactly what dentists always do. Now, go on! Tell me the whole thing. I may mention that I have always suspected you of being a confirmed and secret Bunburyist; and I am quite sure of it now.

JACK: Bunburyist? What on earth do you mean by a Bunburyist?

(continued)

You're the Playwright

Expedition Tool

ALGERNON: I'll reveal to you the meaning of that incomparable expression as soon as you are kind enough to inform me why you are Ernest in town and Jack in the country.

JACK: Well, produce my cigarette case first.

ALGERNON: Here it is. [Hands cigarette case.] Now produce your explanation, and pray make it improbable. [Sits on sofa.]

JACK: My dear fellow, there is nothing improbable about my explanation at all. In fact it's perfectly ordinary. Old Mr. Thomas Cardew, who adopted me when I was a little boy, made me in his will guardian to his grand-daughter, Miss Cecily Cardew. Cecily, who addresses me as her uncle from motives of respect that you could not possibly appreciate, lives at my place in the country under the charge of her admirable governess, Miss Prism.

ALGERNON: Where is that place in the country, by the way?

JACK: That is nothing to you, dear boy. You are not going to be invited . . . I may tell you candidly that the place is not in Shropshire.

ALGERNON: I suspected that, my dear fellow! I have Bunburyed all over Shropshire on two separate occasions. Now, go on. Why are you Ernest in town and Jack in the country?

JACK: My dear Algy, I don't know whether you will be able to understand my real motives. You are hardly serious enough. When one is placed in the position of guardian, one has to adopt a very high moral tone on all subjects. It's one's duty to do so. And as a high moral tone can hardly be said to conduce very much to either one's health or one's happiness, in order to get up to town I have always pretended to have a younger brother of the name of Ernest, who lives in the Albany, and gets into the most dreadful scrapes. That, my dear Algy, is the whole truth pure and simple.

ALGERNON: The truth is rarely pure and never simple. Modern life would be very tedious if it were either, and modern literature a complete impossibility!

JACK: That wouldn't be at all a bad thing.

ALGERNON: Literary criticism is not your forte, my dear fellow. Don't try it. You should leave that to people who haven't been at a University. They do it so well in the daily papers. What you really are is a Bunburyist. I was quite right in saying you were a Bunburyist. You are one of the most advanced Bunburyists I know.

JACK: What on earth do you mean?

(continued)

You're the Playwright

Expedition Tool

ALGERNON: You have invented a very useful younger brother called Ernest, in order that you may be able to come up to town as often as you like. I have invented an invaluable permanent invalid called Bunbury, in order that I may be able to go down into the country whenever I choose. Bunbury is perfectly invaluable. If it wasn't for Bunbury's extraordinary bad health, for instance, I wouldn't be able to dine with you at Willis's to-night, for I have been really engaged to Aunt Augusta for more than a week.

JACK: I haven't asked you to dine with me anywhere to-night.

ALGERNON: I know. You are absurdly careless about sending out invitations. It is very foolish of you. Nothing annoys people so much as not receiving invitations.

JACK: You had much better dine with your Aunt Augusta.

ALGERNON: I haven't the smallest intention of doing anything of the kind. To begin with, I dined there on Monday, and once a week is quite enough to dine with one's own relations. In the second place, whenever I do dine there I am always treated as a member of the family, and sent down with either no woman at all, or two. In the third place, I know perfectly well whom she will place me next to, to-night. She will place me next Mary Farquhar, who always flirts with her own husband across the dinner-table. That is not very pleasant. Indeed, it is not even decent . . . and that sort of thing is enormously on the increase. The amount of women in London who flirt with their own husbands is perfectly scandalous. It looks so bad. It is simply washing one's clean linen in public. Besides, now that I know you to be a confirmed Bunburyist I naturally want to talk to you about Bunburying. I want to tell you the rules.

JACK: I'm not a Bunburyist at all. If Gwendolen accepts me, I am going to kill my brother, indeed I think I'll kill him in any case. Cecily is a little too much interested in him. It is rather a bore. So I am going to get rid of Ernest. And I strongly advise you to do the same with Mr. . . . with your invalid friend who has the absurd name.

ALGERNON: Nothing will induce me to part with Bunbury, and if you ever get married, which seems to me extremely problematic, you will be very glad to know Bunbury. A man who marries without knowing Bunbury has a very tedious time of it.

JACK: That is nonsense. If I marry a charming girl like Gwendolen, and she is the only girl I ever saw in my life that I would marry, I certainly won't want to know Bunbury.

ALGERNON: Then your wife will. You don't seem to realise, that in married life three is company and two is none.

(continued)

You're the Playwright

Expedition Tool

JACK: [Sententiously.] That, my dear young friend, is the theory that the corrupt French Drama has been propounding for the last fifty years.

ALGERNON: Yes; and that the happy English home has proved in half the time.

JACK: For heaven's sake, don't try to be cynical. It's perfectly easy to be cynical.

ALGERNON: My dear fellow, it isn't easy to be anything nowadays. There's such a lot of beastly competition about. [The sound of an electric bell is heard.] Ah! that must be Aunt Augusta. Only relatives, or creditors, ever ring in that Wagnerian manner. Now, if I get her out of the way for ten minutes, so that you can have an opportunity for proposing to Gwendolen, may I dine with you to-night at Willis's?

JACK: I suppose so, if you want to.

ALGERNON: Yes, but you must be serious about it. I hate people who are not serious about meals. It is so shallow of them.

Wilde, Oscar. *The Importance of Being Earnest: A Trivial Comedy for Serious People.* 1895.

(continued)

You're the Playwright

Expedition Tool

Taking Notes

Setting

Setting

Characters

Characters	Personality trait	How do you know?

(chart continues on next page)

You're the Playwright

Expedition Tool

Characters	Personality trait	How do you know?

(continued)

You're the Playwright

Expedition Tool

Props

Props	Used by which character?	Purpose

You're the Playwright

Off You Go

Activity 1: Into the Future

Goal:	To describe the setting for a play
Materials:	notebook, pencil
Tool:	Sample Settings

Directions

1. Read **Expedition Tool: Sample Settings** to become familiar with how an author sets a scene.

2. Identify the setting for the play you would like to write, which should take place in your community 100 years in the future. Remember that your setting should be a real place in your community that you envision changing for the better.

3. After you have described your setting, share your description with a partner.

4. With your partner, choose one of the settings. Work together to write your play using this setting.

My setting:

_____

_____

_____

_____

_____

_____

_____

_____

_____

_____

_____

You're the Playwright

Expedition Tool

Sample Settings
ILE

a play in one-act

by Eugene O'Neill

Characters

Steward

Ben

Captain Keeney

Second Mate

Mrs. Keeney

Joe

Other Crew

[CAPTAIN KEENEY'S cabin on board the steam whaling ship Atlantic Queen—a small, square compartment, about eight feet high, with a skylight in the centre looking out on the poop deck. On the left (the stern of the ship) a long bench with rough cushions is built in against the wall. In front of the bench, a table. Over the bench, several curtained portholes.]

[In the rear, left, a door leading to the captain's sleeping-quarters. To the right of the door a small organ, looking as if it were brand-new, is placed against the wall.]

[On the right, to the rear, a marble-topped, sideboard. On the sideboard, a woman's sewing-basket. Farther forward, a doorway leading to the companion way, and past the officers' quarters to the main deck.]

[In the centre of the room, a stove. From the middle of the ceiling a hanging lamp is suspended. The walls of the cabin are painted white.]

[There is no rolling of the ship, and the light which comes through the skylight is sickly and faint, indicating one of those gray days of calm when ocean and sky are alike dead. The silence is unbroken except for the measured tread of someone walking up and down on the poop deck overhead.]

[It is nearing two bells—one o'clock—in the afternoon of a day in the year 1895.]

(continued)

You're the Playwright

Expedition Tool

[At the rise of the curtain there is a moment of intense silence. Then the STEWARD enters and commences to clear the table of the few dishes which still remain on it after the CAPTAIN'S dinner. He is an old, grizzled man dressed in dungaree pants, a sweater, and a woolen cap with ear-flaps. His manner is sullen and angry. He stops stacking up the plates and casts a quick glance upward at the skylight; then tiptoes over to the closed door in rear and listens with his ear pressed to the crack. What he hears makes his face darken and he mutters a furious curse. There is a noise from the doorway on the right, and he darts back to the table.]

[BEN enters. He is an over-grown, gawky boy with a long, pinched face. He is dressed in sweater, fur cap, etc. His teeth are chattering with the cold and he hurries to the stove, where he stands for a moment shivering, blowing on his hands, slapping them against his sides, on the verge of crying.]

Reprinted from *The Atlantic Book of Modern Plays*. Ed. Sterling Andrus Leonard. Boston: Atlantic Monthly Press, 1921.

VOICES

a play in one-act

by Hortense Flexner

<u>Characters</u>

Yvonne

The Other

[The main street of Domremy, in front of the shattered church sacred to Jeanne D'Arc. Roofless houses and broken buildings stand huddled in ruins. The place is deserted and silent. From the right comes a peasant girl, Yvonne, finely made and young. She wears a coarse, wool skirt and a gray shawl loosely folded about her shoulders. Taking her way down the sunken street, she pauses before the door of the church and kneels. As she does so, another peasant girl, slight and erect, comes silently from the church. The time is late afternoon in May. The south wind is stirring. Yvonne stands.]

Reprinted from *Representative One-Act Plays by American Authors*. Ed. Margaret Gardner Mayorga. Boston: Little, Brown & Co., 1919.

(continued)

You're the Playwright

Expedition Tool

HIS RETURN

a play in one-act

by Percival Wilde

Characters

Helen Hartley

John Hartley

Sylvia Best

A Maid

TIME

The Summer of 1918

[The nicely furnished boudoir in Mrs. Hartley's home in a small Northwestern town. There are three doors. The central one leads into the hall; that on the right into the interior of the house; that on the left into a bathroom. There is the furniture one would expect; a dressing table, a chaise-lounge, two or three dainty chairs, and a pier-glass at one side. On the dressing table are two large framed photographs.]

[At the rise of the curtain the stage is empty. There is a pause. Then there enters John Hartley, a man of thirty-five or forty, dressed in a Canadian uniform.]

[He is very much excited. He is returning home after an absence of years. He enters as if he expects to find his wife here. She is not. He is disappointed, but he takes visible pleasure in going about the room, identifying the many familiar objects which it contains. He stops abruptly at the sight of two portraits on his wife's dressing table, one of him, one of her. He takes up her picture, deeply affected, and kisses it.]

[There is a pause. Then he hears steps coming, and straightens up expectantly.]

Reprinted from *Eight Comedies for Little Theatres*. Percival Wilde. Boston: Little, Brown, and Co., 1922.

You're the Playwright

Off You Go

Activity 2: Dialogue

Goal:	To learn how to reveal character traits through dialogue
Materials:	pencil
Tool:	Revealing Your Character

Directions

1. Think about different plays you have read and how the authors use dialogue to tell you something about the characters' personalities.

2. As a class, you will create two characters and decide what their personalities are.

3. With a partner, create a dialogue between these two characters. Your dialogue should show what each character is like. For instance, if a character is humorous, you could have that character tell a joke. If a character is serious, you could have him or her hear a joke and not laugh.

4. List each character's name and description in **Expedition Tool: Revealing Your Character.**

5. When you write the dialogue, be sure to write the character's name followed by a colon (:). Then write the words the character will say. Skip a line and write the other character's name, a colon, and that character's response.

6. If you want the characters to perform some action, such as walking across the room or picking up an object, write the action inside parentheses and place it before the character's words.

7. Share your dialogue according to your teacher's instructions. Be prepared to explain what you did to reveal each character's traits.

8. Provide feedback to other students. Remember to give positive, constructive comments.

9. Look back at your dialogue. Could you have used any additional props or costumes to help convey the personalities of the characters? If so, what?

_____

_____

_____

_____

_____

Expeditions in Your Classroom: English Language Arts, Grades 6–8   © Walch Education

You're the Playwright

Expedition Tool

Revealing Your Character

Character 1

Name: _____

Description: _____

Personality traits: _____

Character 2

Name: _____

Description: _____

Personality traits: _____

Dialogue:

_____

_____

_____

_____

_____

_____

_____

_____

_____

_____

_____

_____

_____

_____

_____

_____

_____

You're the Playwright

Off You Go

Activity 3: Writing Your Play

Goal:	To create plot, setting, and dialogue for a short play with two characters
Materials:	pencil
Tool:	All the Details

Directions

1. With a partner, begin writing your play about your town 100 years in the future. Use the Expedition Tool to record the details.

2. Write a description of the characters.

3. Write out the setting.

4. Write the dialogue between the characters. Be sure to add any directions for actions they should take in parentheses before the words they will say.

5. When performed, the play should be between 5 and 10 minutes in length.

6. Be sure that the play is able to communicate at least two personality traits of each character. It should also be clear where in your community the conversation is taking place and how that place has changed for the better.

7. *Hint:* It is often easiest to make a rough draft of the conversation. Reread it, and then go back to add words or sentences that help communicate information about the characters and the place.

8. When you are done writing the play, go back and make a list of any props you might need.

9. Reflect on your characters, and decide how their clothing might help communicate their character. Decide on costumes for the characters.

10. Get the costumes and props you will need. Practice reading your play with your partner.

11. If possible, do a dress rehearsal of your skit for your families or friends who are not in the class. See if they can identify at least two personality traits of each character, where the scene takes place, and how the place has changed.

12. Perform your play according to your teacher's instructions.

You're the Playwright

Expedition Tool

All the Details

Characters: _____

_____

_____

_____

_____

_____

_____

_____

Setting: _____

_____

_____

_____

_____

_____

_____

_____

Dialogue: _____

_____

_____

_____

_____

_____

_____

_____

(continued)

You're the Playwright

Expedition Tool

_____

_____

_____

_____

_____

_____

_____

_____

_____

_____

Props: _____

_____

_____

_____

_____

Costumes: _____

_____

_____

_____

_____

You're the Playwright

Check Yourself!

Skill Check

1. In a play, what are acts and scenes?

   _____

   _____

   _____

   _____

2. In a play, what are settings, scenery, and props?

   _____

   _____

   _____

   _____

3. In a play, what is a character? How does a writer create his or her characterization?

   _____

   _____

   _____

   _____

4. In a play, what is dialogue?

   _____

   _____

   _____

   _____

You're the Playwright

Check Yourself!

Self-Assessment and Reflection

Before You Go

❑ I understand the parts of a play, such as acts, scenes, settings, and characters.

Off You Go

❑ I can create a description of a setting in which a play occurs.

❑ I know how writers use dialogue to communicate about the personalities of their characters and the setting.

❑ I can create dialogue that communicates the personality of a character.

Do You Know?

❑ I can define the Lingo to Learn vocabulary terms for this project and give an example of each.

❑ I completed the Skill Check questions and carefully reviewed questions I did not answer correctly.

Reflection

1. What were the most challenging aspects of this project for you and why?

_____

_____

_____

2. Which skills did this project help you develop?

_____

_____

_____

3. If you did this project again, what might you do differently and why?

_____

_____

_____

The Great Debate

Overview

Students will investigate an issue in the community and debate their positions on the best solution.

Time

Total time: 6 to 8 hours

- **Before You Go—Issues of Concern:** one class and 20 minutes of homework, pp. 242–244
- **Activity 1—Forming an Opinion:** four to five classes and 60 minutes of homework, pp. 245–248
- **Check Yourself! Skill Check** and **Self-Assessment and Reflection** worksheets: 30 minutes of class time or homework, pp. 249–251

Materials

- notebook
- news articles
- computers with Internet access
- index cards

Skill Focus

- evaluating media content
- performing research
- thinking critically
- using technology
- writing to persuade
- using presentation skills

Prior Knowledge

- basic grammar and mechanics
- peer editing
- familiarity with forming opinion based on evidence

Team Formation

- Students work in pairs, as individuals, and as a whole class.

The Great Debate

Lingo to Learn—Terms to Know

- **bias:** a way of thinking or an opinion that is affected by a personal belief and not solely dependent upon fact
- **citation:** a recording of the author and source of an idea in a research paper
- **debate:** a format for discussion of two opposing ideas
- **evidence:** facts that support an idea
- **persuasion:** the use of arguments, reasoning, and evidence to change another person's opinion to match your own
- **reasoning:** sequential steps in thinking that lead to an opinion
- **rebuttal:** an opinion stated that challenges the reasoning of another person's argument

Suggested Steps

Preparation

- Review all the materials and activities for the expedition. Note printables that you'll need to copy.
- For at least a week prior to starting the project, have students read news articles online or in the newspaper. Students should bring in articles on issues of concern in their local area. Collect the articles in a notebook in the classroom.
- Arrange for support from the librarian for students doing research on the issues they select.
- It might be helpful to ask the social studies teacher present to the class a discussion on debate and its role in the U.S. political system.
- Do an initial survey on issues that are in the news. Identify which organizations are involved in the issues.

Day 1

1. Distribute **Before You Go: Issues of Concern** (p. 242) and **Expedition Tool: What's the Issue?** (pp. 243–244).

2. Provide students with an overview of the project. They will select two issues that are of concern in their area. They will research the issues and decide on two solutions. Teams of students will debate each issue.

3. Students make a list in the Expedition Tool of issues of local concern that they have read about.

4. Next to each issue, students should identify what organization might be interested in their opinion on the best solution. They might need to refer to the news articles to find this information.

The Great Debate

5. Select two issues for the class to investigate.

6. Create debate teams of three students.

7. Have each team select an issue.

Homework

Have students collect information on the issue their team will be debating. Each student should bring in one article about the issue. They can brainstorm possible solutions to the issue and write them on the Expedition Tool.

Day 2

1. Have members of each debate team share information they have found and the possible solutions to their selected issues.

2. Distribute **Off You Go: Forming an Opinion** (pp. 245–246), along with **Expedition Tool: Debate Guidelines** (p. 247) and **Expedition Tool: Evaluating Web Sites** (p. 248).

3. Review the format for a debate.

4. In their teams, students create a list of steps they need to take to find the best solution to the issue they are investigating.

5. Ask some of the teams to present their ideas, and create a master list of steps. Students copy these steps onto a separate sheet of paper.

6. Students plan how they will research their topic and assign tasks to each team member.

7. Review **Expedition Tool: Evaluating Web Sites.**

8. Review the reasons for checking the reliability of Web sites and citing sources.

9. Allow students to work on their research.

Homework

Students should continue the steps in their preparation for the debate.

Day 3

1. Allow students to continue their research.

2. When the teams have collected the information they need, they decide what the best solution to the problem is. This is the team's position statement.

The Great Debate

3. Each team writes their position statement on an index card and posts it in the room. This will allow opposing teams to identify what their opponents are proposing so that they may build their rebuttal.

4. After writing the position statement, students write their evidence (the facts) that support their opinion on the best solution. They should also record the sources of their facts.

5. Meet with each team to discuss their progress.

6. After all the teams have posted their position statements, share them with the class.

7. Each team identifies the position statements that will oppose their view of the best solution.

8. On the Expedition Tool, students list reasons why they think their opponent's ideas are not the best. Have them record any evidence that supports this view.

9. Teams should then decide who will present each part of the debate: the opening, the supporting evidence, and the closing/rebuttal.

10. Each student outlines his or her segment of the debate.

Homework
Students should continue to do their research and prepare their portion of the debate.

Day 4
1. Students present their segments of the debate to their team members.

2. The students edit one another's segments to assure that the writing is clear, brief, and contains adequate evidence to support their opinions.

3. Teams read their portions of the debate out loud to make sure that they are within the allotted time.

4. Have students review Part 2 of **Expedition Tool: Debate Guidelines** (p. 247), which lists good presentation skills.

5. Allow teams to practice their presentations.

Day 5
1. Conduct the debates. If possible, invite parents and representatives from the appropriate community organizations to attend.

2. After each debate, have each student in the audience write on an index card what they liked about the presentation.

The Great Debate

3. The audience can then be given a short time period in which they can ask the teams questions.

4. When all presentations on an issue are completed, have students vote on which solution they think is the best.

5. Present the position statements to the organizations that are working on the solution.

Final Day

1. Have students complete the **Check Yourself! Skill Check** questions (p. 249–250).

2. Check and review answers.

3. Have students complete the **Check Yourself! Self-Assessment and Reflection** worksheet (p. 251) and submit it (optional).

Project Management Tips and Notes

• Many students have not had experience with debating. They might view it as a time to argue. The purpose is to create rational opinions based on good evidence. Students should focus on the evidence that supports their ideas, not the personalities of their opponents or the quality of the other teams' presentations.

• The success of the project relies in part on how well the issues are selected. The problems researched should be small enough for students to be able to conceptualize a specific solution, but large enough that they can find information on the Internet that supports their solution. For instance, the area may be having trouble with trash removal. Students can research the issue of trash removal on a national level and find that many places are encouraging recycling. Students would then be able to suggest a way the town could encourage this practice following what other towns have done. Alternatively, students might identify global warming as a problem. This might be too large an issue to tackle, as there are so many aspects to it. Students could select one problem related to global warming, such as reduced water supply, and create a solution from there.

Suggested Assessment

Use the Project Assessment Rubric or the following point system:

Team and class participation	15 points
Activity 1	15 points
Activity 2	35 points
Student debate	30 points
Self-Assessment and Reflection	5 points

The Great Debate

Extension Activities

- Students can write a research paper on the issue presenting all of the options.
- Students can make a presentation at the organization working on the issue.
- Students can create a flyer that presents their opinion to the public.

Common Core State Standards Connection

Writing: Text Types and Purposes

W.6.1, W.7.1, W.8.1. Write arguments to support claims with clear reasons and relevant evidence.

Writing: Research to Build and Present Knowledge

W.6.8. Gather relevant information from multiple print and digital sources; assess the credibility of each source; and quote or paraphrase the data and conclusions of others while avoiding plagiarism and providing basic bibliographic information for sources.

W.7.8, W.8.8. Gather relevant information from multiple print and digital sources, using search terms effectively; assess the credibility and accuracy of each source; and quote or paraphrase the data and conclusions of others while avoiding plagiarism and following a standard format for citation.

Speaking and Listening: Comprehension and Collaboration

SL.6.1, SL.7.1, SL.8.1. Engage effectively in a range of collaborative discussions (one-on-one, in groups, and teacher-led) with diverse partners on … topics, texts, and issues, building on others' ideas and expressing their own clearly.

   b. Follow rules for collegial discussions … and define individual roles as needed.*

Speaking and Listening: Presentation of Knowledge and Ideas

SL.6.4. Present claims and findings, sequencing ideas logically and using pertinent descriptions, facts, and details to accentuate main ideas or themes; use appropriate eye contact, adequate volume, and clear pronunciation.

SL.7.4. Present claims and findings, emphasizing salient points in a focused, coherent manner with pertinent descriptions, facts, details, and examples; use appropriate eye contact, adequate volume, and clear pronunciation.

SL.8.4. Present claims and findings, emphasizing salient points in a focused, coherent manner with relevant evidence, sound valid reasoning, and well-chosen details; use appropriate eye contact, adequate volume, and clear pronunciation.

The Great Debate

Language: Conventions of Standard English

L.6.1, L.7.1, L.8.1. Demonstrate command of the conventions of standard English grammar and usage when writing or speaking.

Language: Knowledge of Language

L.6.3, L.7.3, L.8.3. Use knowledge of language and its conventions when writing, speaking, reading, or listening.

Answer Key

Check Yourself! Skill Check

1. Bias is expressed when a personal belief affects the way information is presented. Many Web sites contain biased opinions. They are not based on sound facts. It is important to check the credentials of the person authoring a Web site.

2. A citation credits the original author of an idea. To make a citation, you record the name of the Web site, the author, and the Web address.

3. A debate occurs when two people or teams choose opposing positions on an issue. They present their opinions in a formal sequence for a set amount of time. A rebuttal is the portion of the debate when one team is able to say why they believe the opinion of the other team is not correct.

4. Reasoning is the process of thinking through the sequence of ideas that form an opinion. Critical thinking involves both reasoning through your own opinion and evaluating the opinions of others.

5. Evidence that supports your ideas is an important tool in persuasive writing. If you can state facts that support your opinion, it makes the opinion more believable to others.

6. You should look up from your papers and speak to the audience. You should speak loudly and clearly. You should try not to speak in one tone.

The Great Debate

Expedition Overview

Challenge
Get ready to make your case! You will investigate an issue in your area, research the facts, and form an opinion. Then you will debate the issue with classmates.

Objectives
- To learn about a local issue of concern in your area
- To research the issue and find out possible solutions to the problem
- To work on a debate team to present your position statement supported with evidence and rebut other ideas

Project Activities
Before You Go
- Issues of Concern

Off You Go
- Activity 1: Forming an Opinion

Expedition Tools
- What's the Issue?
- Debate Guidelines
- Evaluating Web Sites

Other Materials Needed
- notebook
- news articles
- computer with Internet access
- index card

Lingo to Learn—Terms to Know
- bias
- citation
- debate
- evidence
- persuasion
- reasoning
- rebuttal

Expeditions in Your Classroom: English Language Arts, Grades 6–8   © Walch Education

The Great Debate

Expedition Overview

Helpful Web Resources

- Cornell University Library—Evaluating Web Sites: Criteria and Tools
  http://olinuris.library.cornell.edu/ref/research/webeval.html

- International Debate Education Association—Teaching Resources
  www.idebate.org/teaching/index.php

- Judge's Decision—For the sample debate on Television is a Bad Influence
  http://video.google.com/videoplay?docid=23820213755448633337&hl=en

- Middle School Public Debate Program—Student Resource Center
  www.middleschooldebate.com/resources/studentresources.htm

(continued)

The Great Debate

Before You Go

Issues of Concern

Goal:	To identify issues of concern in your area and possible solutions
Materials:	notebook
Tool:	What's the Issue?

Directions

1. In the **What's the Issue? Expedition Tool,** make a list of local issues that you have read about online or in the newspaper.

2. For each issue, find the name of any organization that might be interested in your opinion on the topic and the possible solutions you come up with. You will probably find such information in the news articles about the issues.

3. As a class, you will select two issues for the debate teams to investigate and debate.

4. Select one issue that your team will debate.

5. Find one additional article to bring to class about the issue your team will be debating.

6. In the Expedition Tool, make a list of possible solutions for your issue.

The Great Debate

Expedition Tool

What's the Issue?
Local Issues of Concern

Local issue	Organizations involved

(continued)

The Great Debate

Expedition Tool

Issue selected to debate:

_____

_____

_____

Possible solutions:

_____

_____

_____

_____

_____

Expeditions in Your Classroom: English Language Arts, Grades 6–8

The Great Debate

Off You Go

Activity 1: Forming an Opinion

Goal:	To learn how to form a position statement for a debate
Materials:	notebook, computer with Internet access, index card
Tools:	Debate Guidelines, Evaluating Web Sites

Directions

1. Review the format for a debate in Part 1 of **Expedition Tool: Debate Guidelines.**

2. On a separate sheet of paper, make a list of steps your team will need to complete to find the best solution to the issue you are investigating.

3. Discuss this with your class and create a master list of steps. Copy these steps on a separate sheet of paper.

4. Meet with your debate team to plan how you will research the selected topic. Each team member should have a specific task.

5. Review **Expedition Tool: Evaluating Web Sites.**

6. Research your issue. Record your notes, being sure to write the Web page title, author's name, and Web address along with the information.

7. After your team has investigated possible solutions to your selected issue, choose the best solution.

8. Write a statement that describes your solution. This will be your position statement.

9. Write the position statement on an index card and post it in your classroom.

10. On a separate sheet of paper, write the evidence (the facts) you have found that support your opinion on what is the best solution.

11. Be sure you have recorded the sources of these facts.

12. Identify any position statements from other teams that will oppose your opinion of the best solution.

13. Write your rebuttal—the reasons why you think the other solutions are not as good as yours.

14. Note any evidence that supports this view.

The Great Debate

Off You Go

15. As a team, decide who will present each part of the debate: the opening, the supporting evidence, and the closing/rebuttal.

16. Outline and then write your segment of the debate.

17. Share your segment of the debate with your team members and receive feedback.

18. Practice reading your part of the debate. Make sure that you are within the allotted time.

19. Review Part 2 of **Expedition Tool: Debate Guidelines,** which lists good presentation skills. Practice your presentation.

20. Conduct the debate according to your teacher's instructions.

Expeditions in Your Classroom: English Language Arts, Grades 6–8 © Walch Education

The Great Debate

Expedition Tool

Debate Guidelines

Part 1: Debate Format

Team A—Solution 1

Team B—Solution 2

Team C—Solution 3

Team D—Solution 4

Team A: Position statement (3 minutes)

Team A: Evidence in support of position (3 minutes)

Team B: Position statement (3 minutes)

Team B: Evidence in support of position (3 minutes)

Team C: Position statement (3 minutes)

Team C: Evidence in support of position (3 minutes)

Team D: Position statement (3 minutes)

Team D: Evidence in support of position (3 minutes)

Break for each team to form summary (3 minutes)

Questions to any team from the audience (5 minutes)

Team A: Summary statement (3 minutes)

Team B: Summary statement (3 minutes)

Team C: Summary statement (3 minutes)

Team D: Summary statement (3 minutes)

Part 2: Good Presentation Skills
- Speak slowly and clearly so the audience can understand you.
- Speak loudly so all can hear.
- Look up from your papers at the audience.
- Hold your papers still, or place them on a stand.
- Stand up straight.
- Speak with variation in your tone to add emotion or emphasis.

The Great Debate

Expedition Tool

Evaluating Web Sites

Anyone can post information on the Internet. Not all the facts posted online are accurate. It is important that you look at who created a Web site to be certain the information is not biased or unreliable.

- Examine the URL, or the Web address. If the address ends in *.gov,* the site is sponsored by the government. If the address ends in *.edu,* the site is sponsored by a school or university. These are the two types of sites that have the most reliable information. If it is not one of those, you will need to investigate further.
- Find who wrote the page. Look for a tab or link such as "about the" organization. Here you will probably find information about the person or organization that made the page.
- Look to see if the Web page shows the date on which it was last updated. The date is usually at the very bottom of the Web page. If the page hasn't been updated for a while, the information might no longer be accurate.

Citing References

When you find information on a Web page, it is important that you give credit to the author for the idea. You should note the page title, the author's name, the date you accessed the information, and the Web address. Here is an example of how to cite a Web page:

Central Intelligence Agency. "The World Factbook: Korea, South." U.S. Central Intelligence Agency. https://www.cia.gov/library/publications/the-world-factbook/geos/ks.html (accessed January 18, 2012).

The Great Debate

Check Yourself!

Skill Check

1. What is bias? Why is it important to check that a Web site has reliable information?

_____

_____

_____

_____

2. What does it mean to make a citation when conducting research?

_____

_____

_____

_____

3. What is a debate? What does it mean to make a rebuttal?

_____

_____

_____

_____

4. What roles do reasoning and critical thinking play in a debate?

_____

_____

_____

_____

(*continued*)

The Great Debate

Check Yourself!

5. Why is using evidence important when you are trying to persuade others?

_____

_____

_____

_____

6. What are some important things to keep in mind when making a presentation?

_____

_____

_____

_____

The Great Debate

Check Yourself!

Self-Assessment and Reflection

Before You Go

❑ I understand how to identify issues of local concern.

Off You Go

❑ I know how to research issues to find possible solutions.

❑ I know how to check Web sites for reliability.

❑ I know how to create a good position statement for a debate.

❑ I know how to present a debate.

Do You Know?

❑ I can define the Lingo to Learn vocabulary terms for this project and give an example of each.

❑ I completed the Skill Check questions and carefully reviewed questions I did not answer correctly.

Reflection

1. What were the most challenging aspects of this project for you and why?

   _____

   _____

   _____

2. Which skills did this project help you develop?

   _____

   _____

   _____

3. If you did this project again, what might you do differently and why?

   _____

   _____

   _____